T0209751

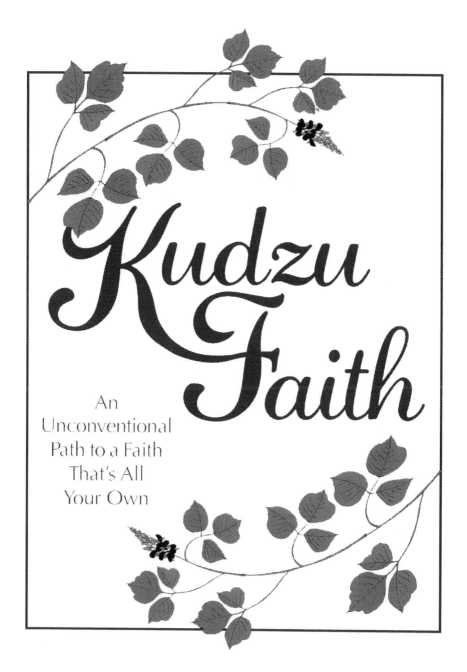

Kudzu Faith

An Unconventional Path to a Faith That's All Your Own

Donette Bayne

WESTBOW
PRESS®
A DIVISION OF THOMAS NELSON
& ZONDERVAN

WestBow Press books may be ordered through
booksellers or by contacting:

WestBow Press
A Division of Thomas Nelson & Zondervan
1663 Liberty Drive
Bloomington, IN 47403
www.westbowpress.com
1 (866) 928-1240

ISBN: 978-1-9736-8123-6 (sc)
ISBN: 978-1-9736-8125-0 (hc)
ISBN: 978-1-9736-8124-3 (e)

Library of Congress Control Number: 2019919758

Print information available on the last page.

WestBow Press rev. date: 12/11/2019

Dedication

To my husband, Randall – No one has ever believed in me,
supported me and challenged me the way you do.
Thank you for never giving up on me and loving
me enough to push—even when I didn't want to go!
I never knew love could be this grand!

To Al and John – the best gifts God could have given me.
You are the children of my heart
and nothing I've done or will ever do will
means more to me than being your extra "mom."
I cherish you both and constantly thank God
for allowing me to share your lives.

To Ken – I thank God that you're my brother.
And more than that, I thank Him that you're my friend.
I love you Bubba and am so very proud of you!

Introduction

I have a calling. Well, we all do. God didn't create a single person without creating within them a unique calling, a purpose that is uniquely theirs. So, yes, I have a calling.

I have been a Christian since I was 13. Most of those years, I lived the Christian life my church and my parents told me to live. I never questioned or challenged the beliefs that were handed down to me. Very few of us do. So, we often wind up trying to live out someone else's faith and not our own. I know I did.

Twice God has stopped me and forced me to examine what I believed and why I believed it. The first time, I was young and heartbroken by life and my choices. I spent almost six months grappling with my beliefs. The struggle got me on the road to my own church, my own faith, my own worship. And I followed along that path for many years.

Then, in 2009, I hit a benchmark, a crisis in faith. A battle of epic proportions began between God and me. A lifetime of hurts, disappointments, regrets, fears, and anger reached a crescendo and I found myself unable to escape or hide from the pain and confusion and turmoil that filled my heart and mind and soul.

The battle was long—almost four years. It alternated between seasons of agonizing prayer and sorrow and times of such anger that I did not speak to or seek anything from God. The journey during that time was dark, ugly, profound, joyful, heartbreaking, and finally, freeing.

My faith became mine, founded and embedded in God's calling and imprint on my life. It is not a traditional evangelical faith, nor is it always recognizable to my "church" friends as their kind of faith. And that's okay.

One of the results of this transformation has been the amazing gift God has given me—my husband. He is a man of intense, individualized faith, a man called by God to walk a very nontraditional path. And I would have run away from him so quickly had God not brought me to a new faith, a new walk. Over these past years, I've come to understand so much more about this path on which God has placed me as Randall and I walk our life together.

There is still a battle being fought in my heart and mind and soul. God's calling, His purpose for me, is right here in front of me. For years, I caught small glimpses, snippets of it. And it excited me and terrified me. So, as we "good" Christians so often do, I ran from it. I distanced myself, I turned from or ignored God. I had a very "push me, pull me" attitude and I stayed way too long in that unfulfilled, safe, frustrating place.

But in 2015, for the first time in ages, I made a New Year's resolution. No more running, hiding, avoiding, or ignoring. I turned my face, heart, soul, and mind toward the God Who called me out, wrestled with me in the dark, and won my heart. I began to step willingly into His call and purpose for my life.

Even after all this time, such trepidation fills me even as I write these words. But those are the fears and doubts of the old creature. The new creature, the child throwing open her arms in love and trust will, by God's grace, move past the fears into her new, glorious walk with my Lord.

So, this is the second amazing result of God's transformation in my life, leading me into my calling, these words I've placed on paper, prayerfully committing the inspirations and thoughts

God has placed on my heart out here for all to read. I hope as you move through these observations, these soul-deep honest writings, that you will read something that touches your heart and soul. I pray that, if you haven't already, you will begin to look for your own calling, to find that wonderfully fulfilling, blessed place God has called you to enter. I hope and pray that your faith will be strengthened, your eyes opened and your heart filled.

Enjoy and may your own kudzu faith begin to take over.

Faith Like Kudzu

"For everyone born of God overcomes the world. This is the victory that has overcome the world, even our faith." I John 5:4 (NIV)[1]

Growing up in the South, we had an age-old Sunday afternoon tradition. After church, we would load up in the car and head "to the country" to visit family. Along the way, we would drive past fields and meadows, full of ripening crops and blooming flowers.

And kudzu. Lots and lots of kudzu.

For those of you not from the deep, sunny South, let me introduce you to kudzu.

According to Wikipedia, kudzu, or Japanese Arrowroot, as it's known in more sophisticated circles, was introduced to the US in 1876 at the Centennial Exposition in Philadelphia and in the 1930s and 1940s was reintroduced and rebranded as a way for farmers to stop soil erosion. In the early days, railroad and highway developers also used it to stop erosion along the paths they were carving in the country's landscape. It grows primarily in the South, and apparently really, really loves Southern soil. According to some reports, it can spread at a rate of 150,000 acres a year; however, in 2015, the US

Forest Service estimated it spreads at a rate of only (*only!?!?*) 2,500 acres per year.

Kudzu quickly covers everything in its path and is incredibly hard to kill. It competes with native plants for light and blocks their access to sunlight by growing over them and shading them with its leaves, causing them to die as a result.

Oddly enough, there have been those who revered this invasive vine. In the 1940s, there was a fellow named Channing Cope, a popular radio host, who created something of a cult following for kudzu. He even started the Kudzu Club of America, with membership of over 20,000. [2]

These days, there are kudzu festivals and kudzu queens all over the South. We Southerners are really big on throwing a party for just about anything, the weirder the better. We have come to embrace the craziness that is kudzu, and see its growth as sort of a badge of honor, as it envelopes old abandoned houses, barns, and cars. Nowadays, we see kudzu as a way to cover the ugly.

As a child traveling around the countryside with my Daddy, my brothers and I were exposed to the legends of kudzu that have intrigued and, to some extent, terrified, all Southerners. According to Daddy, kudzu was a monster crop sent to the US to slowly (or not so slowly) destroy us. Cattle wouldn't eat it, nothing could stop its advance across the land. As we stared out the car windows, wide-eyed and a bit nervous, Daddy would warn us that kudzu could overtake a power pole, a field, barn, and maybe even slow-moving cattle in no time at all. We were told nothing good could ever come from kudzu; it was the curse the South would just have to endure.

Nowadays, I rarely notice kudzu as I drive along back roads and interstates. It's as much a part of my heritage as hot, muggy summer days, and those weird festivals.

But recently, for some inexplicable reason, God started using kudzu to talk to me about faith. Leave it to Him to use something as odd as kudzu to get my attention.

God pointed out that, as crazy as it may seem, kudzu is a lot like our faith.

Kudzu spreads and takes over everything in its path. As we grow as Christians, our faith should have that same power. Through Christ, our faith will consume and smother all the "ugly" that has filled us. And as our faith grows, others will see its strength and its power to overcome.

"For everyone who has been born of God overcomes the world. And this is the victory that has overcome the world—our faith." I John 5:4 (ESV)[3]

Kudzu prevents erosion. Through its deep root system, it holds together that in which it's planted and accomplishes its purpose. It holds steady in the storms that hit it, never letting what's underneath wash away. Our faith, grounded in Christ, will hold us steady no matter the storms. Our faith will accomplish that for which it is intended. Our faith will accomplish its purpose in our lives.

"Therefore, my dear brothers and sisters, stand firm. Let nothing move you." I Corinthians 15:58a (NIV)

"So that Christ may dwell in your hearts through faith— that you, being rooted and grounded in love, may have strength to comprehend with all the saints what is the breadth and length and height and depth, and to know the love of Christ that surpasses knowledge, that you may be filled with the fullness of God." Ephesians 3:17-19 (ESV)

Kudzu is strong. Nothing seems to be able to defeat it. There is really nothing that kudzu can't overcome. And our faith, as it grows, is the same. We will have the power to stand firm, the power to grow and serve, the power to show the world the might of our Savior.

"For truly I tell you, if you have faith as small as a mustard seed, you can say to this mountain, 'Move from here to there,' and it will move. Nothing will be impossible for you." Matthew 17:20b (NIV)

As hard as it may be for a Southerner to say, we need to embrace kudzu. Our faith should reflect the strength and resilience of kudzu. We should stand firm, overcome, and have a faith that is never eroded. We should grow where we are planted, covering all around us with the power of our faith in Christ.

So, the next time you're riding down a Southern country road, notice the kudzu. See how it has conquered all around it, how it has claimed all the land. And remember that God has filled each of us with the faith to do the same—the faith like kudzu.

Count It All What??

"And after you have suffered for a little while, the God of all grace, who has called you to His eternal glory in Christ, will Himself restore, confirm, strengthen, and establish you." I Peter 5:10 (ESV)

Not long after I started college, while enduring that age-old rite of passage—working part-time retail—I met the Executive Vice President of our local hometown bank. After a pretty witty exchange, he offered me a job. I accepted on the condition that I never again had to work with "the public," and for the next three and a half years he did his best to honor my request.

I was assigned to the proofing department, a room above the lobby of the bank filled with an enormous, phenomenally loud prehistoric machine that balanced deposits and printed the magnetic numbers on the checks and deposit slips. Those of you who have never lived without a laptop or handheld device have no idea how far we've come!

My supervisor was a woman named Sylvia. Sylvia was from Michigan, smoked like a freight train, talked with a deep, raspy smoker's voice and although we never heard it, undoubtedly cussed like a drunken sailor when she was away from the office. I had never, in my sheltered Southern Pentecostal upbringing met anyone like her.

I adored her.

Sylvia took me under her wing and taught me the ropes of her domain, the proofing department. It was my first experience with an adult who encouraged me and believed in my ability to learn and do anything that was put before me. I thrived in that part-time job in that little bank.

But occasionally I would come in and Sylvia would greet with me a new assignment.

"Today," she would say, "you get a new learning experience."

The first time that happened, Sylvia explained to me that 1) new learning experiences can't be avoided; and 2) they are never fun.

She was not wrong.

As the years have progressed, my life and my Christian walk have been filled with many new learning experiences. Almost without exception, Sylvia's description has held true. The experiences can't be avoided and, to date, none of them have been what I'd—or any sane person—would call fun. The learning experiences in life have for the most part stunk. Heartbreaks; heavy financial responsibilities; getting and keeping a good job; dealing with break-ups, betrayals, and death. Some have been short-lived; some have felt as if they lasted forever. Each provided an unavoidable learning experience. None were fun.

James tells us in Chapter 1: 2-4 (NIV), *"Consider it pure joy, my brothers and sisters, whenever you face trials of many kinds, because you know that the testing of your faith produces perseverance. Let perseverance finish its work so that you may be mature and complete, not lacking anything."*

Okay, I've been a Christian a lot of years. I'd had my share of trials. I can say, with complete honesty, that I have not, one single time, considered it joy, pure or otherwise. Painful? Yes. Aggravating, frustrating and completed unwanted? Absolutely.

Pure joy? No way, no how.

I have encountered those lovely saints who, in the midst of great trials and tribulations, have smiled and quoted some scripture like Romans 8:28 (NIV), *"And we know that all things work together for the good of those who love Him, who have been called according to His purpose."*

We've all met those people. Maybe you're one of them.

When I hear this, I smile and nod and agree. But inside, I kinda want to punch them in the nose.

I've lived long enough and experienced enough of my own trials and tribulations and pain and heartbreak to know that Romans 8:28 is in fact true. I even know that James 1: 2-4 is true.

Doesn't mean I don't still kinda want to punch them in the nose.

When my trials hit, Romans 8:28 has never been my initial, early—or sometimes ever—response. I wish that it was. I wish that, after the initial shock of—again—getting hit by the painful new "learning experience" I could stop, turn my eyes toward Jesus and cling to Romans 8:28 and James 1: 2-4.

"All things work together for good" (Romans 8:28 NIV)

"So that you may be mature and complete, not lacking anything" (James 1:4 NIV)

I know I should, as Paul tell us, rejoice in our suffering. According to Paul, suffering results in all kinds of great stuff: perseverance, character, hope. I get it. I just don't like it.

I have been known, during times of trial, while going through yet another "learning experience," to inform God that I am perfectly content being an immature Christian, with faith as shallow as a mud puddle. He never listens to me.

Instead, He keeps putting me in the middle of these trying experiences and I somehow do manage to learn something, usually in spite of myself.

Learning experiences, or trials as James calls them, are as much a part of life as breathing and eating. We can't avoid them. All we can do is decide how we're going to face and walk through them.

Years ago, I came across a book entitled *You're Late Again, Lord! The Impatient Woman's Guide to God's Timing*, by Karon Phillips Goodman.[4] I bought the book because the title was catchy. I read it because every page contained truths that stomped all over my toes. One of the most powerful truths I found in the book was this: we keep going through this stuff—the trials, the testing, the learning experiences—because we fail to learn the lessons God is trying to teach us.

I don't know about you, but many times I come out of these times with nothing but relief that I survived. Not, as James and Paul talked about, with perseverance and maturity and completeness and character and hope. Nope, I come out with gratitude that it's over or even sometimes resentment and anger that it happened at all.

Wow, just writing that makes me understand why the trials and life lessons keep coming! I'm a really slow learner!

It's been said that the definition of insanity is doing the same thing over and over expecting a different outcome.

That could also be the definition of spiritual immaturity. Ouch.

The good news, if you can call it that, is I'm pretty sure that neither Paul nor James got this right the first time around. That gives me hope. And, Hebrews 13:5b (NIV) reminds us that God has said, *"Never will I leave you; never will I forsake you,"* so I know that no matter how long it takes me to get it right, He'll stick with me.

I guess I'm in good company. The Bible is full of those who were slow to learn, who ran from God, who complained and whined and fussed. And yet God found a way to teach them and use them. So, I'll keep trying. I'll keep facing those no-fun, aggravating "learning experiences" and I'll, hopefully, with God's help and infinite grace, grow.

And maybe, just maybe, I'll start counting it all joy.

Seek

"Ask and it will be given to you; seek and you will find; knock and the door will be opened. For everyone who asks receives, the one who seeks finds; and to the one who knocks, the door will be opened." Matthew 7:7-8 (NIV)

For most Christians, these verses are as familiar as John 3:16. Sermons are preached. Books are written. We may even have cute little plaques or coffee mugs with the verses emblazoned on them. We cling to the promises of scripture and these are cornerstone verses.

During our short marriage, my husband and I have lived through some pretty rough places. During these times, we found ourselves alternating between borderline terror and thankfulness for God's provision. It was exhausting, emotionally, mentally, and professionally, filled with optimism and discouragement.

And spiritually, it was overwhelming. There were days of rejoicing; there were many, many days of crying out in disappointment and desperation. Almost all days contained thanks and praise, even when in our humanness, we weren't sure why we were thanking and praising.

During one of these times, I decided to pray and claim the promises of God, so I pulled out pen and paper and started writing them down. There are **lots** of them. I mean, the Bible is packed full of promises, many spoken by Jesus during His time here on earth, about God's provision and our protection.

I wrote down almost 20 promises and there have been many days when I have read them back to Jesus and the Father, claiming them and thanking Heaven for them.

Matthew 7:7 is the first verse on my list. If I asked each of you to make a list, it would probably be close to the top of yours, too.

But recently, when I read it, there was this strange catch in my spirit, as if God was trying to point my attention to something. I kept hearing one word repeat over and over in my heart:

Seek.

And I realized there is something very different about that middle phrase.

There are lots of verses in the Bible about asking and receiving:

"If you believe, you will receive whatever you ask for in prayer." Matthew 21:22 (NIV)

"And I will do whatever you ask in my name, so that the Father may be glorified in the Son." John 14:13 (NIV)

"You do not have because you do not ask." James 4:2b (ESV)

There are parables about knocking: the widow and unjust judge; the persistent friend banging on the neighbor's door at midnight.

But seeking? Verses that talk about seeking all have a different focus:

"You will seek me and find me when you seek me with all your heart." Jeremiah 29:13 (NIV)

"Seek the Lord while He may be found; call on Him while He is near." Isaiah 55:6 (NIV)

"But seek first the Kingdom of God and His righteousness, and all these things will be added to you." Matthew 6:33 (ESV)

"And without faith it is impossible to please Him, for he who comes to God must believe that He is and that He is a rewarder of those who seek Him." (Hebrews 11:6) (NASB)[5]

How many times have we read Matthew 7:7? How many times have we prayed, "Okay God, I'm asking, I'm seeking, I'm knocking. Please answer my prayer."?

What are we seeking? Our answer, our need met, yes. But are we seeking God? Because, according to these scriptures, we should.

I—we—got so caught up in seeking the answer, we forget to seek the Answer Giver.

Matthew 6:33 and Hebrews 11:6 indicate that most of the time we get it backwards. We seek our answer, figuring it will bring us closer to God when we get it. These verses make it pretty clear we're supposed to seek **God** and His Kingdom and **then** we'll get the answer.

Psalm 37:4 (ESV) says, *"Delight yourself in the Lord and he will give you the desires of your heart."*

It **does not** say, "He will give you the desires of your heart and then you will delight yourself in the Lord."

But that's how we pray. That's how we live.

I've been pretty convicted about this. I realize I've been so focused on our needs and requests that I've taken my focus off the Father. When I think about Him, most of the time it's as my Provider, the Answer to my prayers.

And He is. But, oh, He is so much more!

Jeremiah 9:24 (ESV) tells us, *"But let him who boasts boast in this, that he knows and understands Me, that I am the Lord who practices steadfast love, justice and righteousness in the earth. For in these things I delight, declares the Lord."*

I want to be able to boast that I know and understand Him. But if all I do is bring my list of requests to Him, remind Him again of my needs, give Him His marching orders and say "amen," how will I ever know or understand Him?

He has lessons for us to learn during the struggles and challenges we face. He wants us to learn **Him**, to grow closer to Him, to understand more about His character and personality. That's the reason we go through these hard times. And one thing's for sure—we'll keep going through them, often because we failed to learn what He was trying to teach us.

I want to do better. I want to seek **Him** and His Kingdom. I want to know and understand **Him** more.

So, while I'm asking and knocking, I'm going to seek. I'm going to seek God's face. I'm going to seek to know Him more. I'm going to seek His voice.

I'm going to keep banging on the door. I'm going to keep asking until the answer comes.

But I'm also going to pray, as Samuel did so long ago,

"Speak, for Your servant is listening." I Samuel 3:10b (NIV)

And in the asking and knocking, He will be found in my seeking.

Learning To Listen

"But the Helper, the Holy Spirit, whom the Father will send in my name, He will teach you everything and will remind you of everything I have told you." John 14:26 (ESV)

"I bought you something for breakfast," my sweet husband announced as he delivered my coffee. I had already seen the box of turnovers on the kitchen counter.

"Thank you, honey, but I really don't like them," I reply, gently rejecting his kind gesture.

After a moment, I hear, "Huh. Well, I guess I won't buy those again."

I walk into the kitchen a few minutes later to find a non-turnover breakfast, thinking of the other times we've had almost the same conversation. He comes home with a box of turnovers, apple, cherry, whatever fruit, expressing his love for me with this thoughtful gift. And me, gently reminding him, once again, that I don't like them.

'We've been married nearly four years,' I think as I forage for an alternative breakfast. 'I've told him over and over I don't like them. It's like he doesn't even hear me.'

And then it happened. Right in front of the stove, my package of cookies (don't judge) gripped in my hand.

That sweet, still voice whispers:

'Yeah, I know how you feel.'

Well, that was convicting.

Despite what Philippians 4:6-7 (NIV) says, *"Don't worry about anything; instead pray about everything. Tell God what you need and thank Him for all He has done. Then you will experience God's peace, which exceeds anything we can understand. His peace will guard your hearts and minds as you live in Christ Jesus,"* most mornings, before my eyes even open, my mind is filled with all the worries and fears of what could go wrong in our day.

Instead of *"Be still (cease striving) and know that I am God,"* Psalm 46:10 (ESV), I immediately start stressing over circumstances and people I can't control.

The Bible is full of verses that tell us—command us—to not worry, to "fear not." And yet I—we—do.

I don't listen. I don't hear.

In John 10:27 (ESV), Jesus said, *"My sheep hear my voice and I know them, and they follow me."*

Sheep aren't born knowing the shepherd's voice. It takes time. It takes hearing his voice, over and over, before they recognize it, associate it with safety, and follow it.

We are the same way. It takes time in the presence of our Shepherd to learn to hear His voice, associate it with safety, and follow it.

Before Jesus ascended, He promised the disciples that He would send the Holy Spirit to teach them and **remind them** of everything Jesus had told them (John 14:26 NIV). That promise is extended to us also as followers of Christ. The problem isn't that He's not speaking; the problem is that I don't hear. I let the day's worries overwhelm me before my feet even hit the floor.

Matthew 6: 31, 33-34 (ESV) directs us, *"Therefore, do not be anxious, saying, 'What shall we eat?' or 'What shall we drink?' or 'What shall we wear?'. But seek first the Kingdom of God and His righteousness and all these things will be added to you. Therefore, do not be anxious about tomorrow, for tomorrow will anxious for itself. Sufficient for the day is its own trouble."*

Allowing all of these worries to flood my mind and heart will not solve a thing. It will, however, take my focus off the One who can—and has—solved them.

Isaiah 65:24 (NLT)[6] declares, *"I will answer them before they even call to me. While they are still talking about their needs, I will go ahead and answer their prayers!"*

So, I need to hear. I need to "cease striving" and know that He is God. I need to listen to the Holy Spirit and be reminded yet again, before I rise, before the day begins, of this promise:

"The Lord Himself goes before you and will be with you; He will never leave you nor forsake you. Do not be afraid; do not be discouraged." Deuteronomy 31:8 (NIV)

My day will have enough troubles of its own. But the Holy Spirit reminds me of the words of Jesus:

"I have told you these things, so that in Me you may have peace. In the world you will have trouble. But take heart! I have overcome the world." John 16:33 (NIV)

So, before I open my eyes, I will replace my worries with a prayer. I will hear the Holy Spirit's reminder:

"Greater is He that is in you than he who is in the world." I John 4:4b (NASB)

And even as those doubts and fears try to overwhelm, I will remember and sing the words of the old African American spiritual:

> "In the morning when I rise,
> In the morning when I rise,
> In the morning when I rise,
> Give me Jesus"[7]

And I will remember and claim:

> "Turn your eyes upon Jesus
> Look full in His wonderful face.
> And the things of earth will grow strangely dim
> In the light of His glory and grace"[8]

Lessons Of The Bradford Pear

*"But the L*ORD *said to Samuel, 'The L*ORD *does not look at the things people look at. People look at the outward appearance, but the L*ORD *looks at the heart.'"* I Samuel 16:7b (NIV)

It's Springtime in Nashville. New life has arrived. Flowers are blooming, birds are singing, days are longer and warmer.

And Bradford Pear trees are covered in beautiful, delicate white flowers. That really stink. I realize not everyone feels this way. Some people, somehow, love the aroma of those fluffy little stink-pods. I'm not one of those.

Recently, as I rushed inside to avoid breathing in the noxious fumes of the big, blooming trees in my front yard, I thought, 'how can something that pretty smell that bad?' And God gently tapped me on the shoulder and said, "Remind you of anyone?"

Not one of my favorite messages from the Father, but He did, as usual, have a point. We get so concerned with outward appearances, ours and others, that we forget about the inside. We look great, but negative, hurtful words pour out of us. We harbor judgmental, condemning thoughts. The enemy fills our minds with all sorts of things that distract us from the Father and His good and perfect ways.

In Matthew 23:7 (NIV), Jesus said, *"Woe to you, teachers of the law and Pharisees, you hypocrites! You are like whitewashed tombs, which look beautiful on the outside but on the inside are full of the bones of the dead and everything unclean."*

He could have been speaking to any of us, to me. I struggle, more often than I'd like, with battles of the mind. My pettiness and sinfulness are, some days, rampant in my thoughts. My outside is clean and shiny, my inside, not so much.

As I look at the Bradford Pear tree outside my window, I think about the lesson God is trying to teach me: just because I **look** good doesn't mean I **am** good. There are many days I'm just like that tree and its stinky flowers.

Even Paul struggled with this. In Romans 7:15, 24 (NIV), he declared, *"I do not understand what I do. For what I want to do I do not do, but what I hate I do. . . . What a wretched man I am! Who will rescue me from this body that is subject to death?"*

We are all going to struggle with the war that wages in us: the new creation in Christ and the old man. There will be days when we are sure we've lost the battle and no good can remain in us or come out of us. But in verse 25 (NIV), Paul gives us all hope:

"Thanks be to God, who delivers me through Jesus Christ our Lord!"

And John reminds us in I John 1:9 (NIV), *"If we confess our sins, He is faithful and just and will forgive us our sins and purify us from all unrighteousness."*

So I confess. I ask the Father to forgive me and remove all the "stinky flowers" that fill my thoughts and heart. I ask that my "inside me" look as presentable as my "outside me." And I thank Him that He is working to restore Springtime and new life inside me.

All Evidence To The Contrary

I'll show up and take care of you as I promised and bring you back home. I know what I'm doing. I have it all planned out; plans to take care of you, not abandon you, plans to give You the future you hope for. When you call on Me, when you come and pray to Me, I'll listen. When you come looking for Me, you'll find Me. Yes, when you get serious about finding Me and want it more than anything else, I'll make sure you won't be disappointed. Jeremiah 29:11-13 (MSG)[9]

When you're in the desert, praying and waiting for your rescue, you have days when you feel forgotten, when you are sure God's turned off the phone and is ignoring your calls.

Even David felt this way:

"How long, O Lord? Will You forget me forever? How long will you hide Your face from me?" Psalm 13:1 (NIV)

"I am worn out calling for help; my throat is parched. My eyes fail looking for my God." Psalm 69:3 (NIV)

That place of waiting on the Lord can be very lonely. It can be filled with discouragement and doubt. Satan spends a lot of time trying to convince us that we have been forgotten, that God has turned His back on us.

I've been there. I've had days—sometimes weeks—when, if I prayed at all, I felt my words weren't getting past the ceiling.

A friend recently reminded me that our faith is not based on what we see or what we feel but on what we know is true.

God hears, God moves, God answers.

Isaiah 65:24 (NLT) promises, *"I will answer them before they even call on me. While they are still talking about their needs, I will go ahead and answer their prayers!"*

When I'm in that lonely, "I've been forgotten" place, I have a phrase that I find myself repeating over and over: "all evidence to the contrary."

"All evidence to the contrary, God is hearing."

"All evidence to the contrary, God is moving."

"All evidence to the contrary, God is answering."

Our physical eyes often try to tell lies to our spiritual eyes.

I Corinthians 2:9 says (NLT), *"That is what the Scriptures mean when they say, 'No eye has seen, no ear has heard and no mind has imagined what God has prepared for those who love Him.'"*

When we're stuck in this place of waiting, we have to ignore what we see and instead claim what we know, what Scripture declares.

Jeremiah 29:11-13 declares our truth. God knows what He's doing. He has it all worked out. That's His job. Our job is to trust Him, call on Him and seek Him with our whole hearts.

And we have to keep praising. Even when it doesn't make sense to our human minds. Even when we cannot see, with our physical eyes, any reason to praise.

David ends Psalm 13 with these verses:

"But I trust in Your unfailing love; My heart rejoices in Your salvation. I will sing the Lord's praise for He has been good to me." Psalm 13:5-6 (NIV)

And He finishes Chapter 69 declaring:

"I will praise God's name in song and glorify Him with thanksgiving. This will please the Lord more than an ox, more

than a bull with its horns and hooves. The poor will see and be glad—You who seek God, may your hearts live!" Psalm 69:30-32 (NIV)

So, we cling to scripture; we claim His promises. We remember, as David did, that all evidence to the contrary, His unfailing love endures forever.

Suddenly

"When the people heard the sound of the rams' horns, they shouted as loud as they could. **Suddenly,** *the walls of Jericho collapsed, and the Israelites charged straight into the town and captured it."* Joshua 6:20 (NLT, emphasis added)

Suddenly. God can intervene at any time He chooses. Your world can look one way at one moment and completely different the next. All you need is for God to show up in His mighty power.

The walls of Jericho looked exactly the same after the Israelites obediently circled them 13 times. But when everything was in place and everything God told them to do was done, "suddenly" the walls fell.

Never forget the possibility of a "suddenly" from God in your life.

"God, all at once, (suddenly) you turned on a floodlight for me!

You are the revelation light in my darkness and in Your brightness, I can see the path ahead.

With You as my strength I can crush an enemy horde advancing through every stronghold that stands in front of me.

What a God You are!

Your path for me has been perfect!
All Your promises have proven true.
What a secure shelter for all those who turn to hide themselves in You!" Psalm 18: 28-30 (TPT)[10]

Suddenly. It's a word that can fill us with great joy, great anticipation, or great fear.

There are lots of "suddenly" moments in the Bible. And when they happened, those involved always seemed so surprised. But if you read the story surrounding the "suddenly," you always see events that give a lot of clues that "suddenly" was coming.

Years ago, I was in a job I hated. Not just didn't want, but really, really hated. For two and a half years, I prayed for a new job with no results.

Then suddenly. I was asked to move to another city to help open an office, doing the same work that I hated. I didn't want to go and turned down the position. I was told my job description would change and the part of the job I did enjoy would be gone. Then suddenly, I was contacted out of the blue by a former co-worker who knew about a job opening. It was a great job, exactly what I wanted. I applied before the advertisement for the job was even posted. I got an interview right away. I was offered the job the next week. I accepted it and started on the day set for me to take on my new responsibilities at the old job.

Folks who knew me all commented that everything had happened so fast, so suddenly.

What they didn't understand was that it took two and a half years to get to suddenly.

What I took away from this experience was that when we ask God for something, we need to ALWAYS be ready for His answer. He operates in the "Yes" realm; we tend to live in the "what if" realm.

"For no matter how many promises God has made, they are "Yes" in Christ. And so through Him the "Amen" (which means "yes") is spoken by us to the glory of God." II Corinthians 1:20 (NIV, explanation added)

How many "Yes" answers do we miss because we aren't ready to move?

How many times, no matter how hard we've prayed, do we hesitate when the answer appears?

Why do we question the answer? Why do we question God?

We humans want to hedge our bets; we want back-up plans and exit strategies. God just wants us to trust.

God has promised to hear and answer our prayers. Our job is to live in the realm of faith, expectantly anticipating the answer.

We don't know how long it will take for the answer to come. The Jewish nation waited for hundreds of years for the Messiah to come. And then one night He did. And nothing would ever be the same.

"Suddenly, there was with the angel a multitude of the Heavenly host praising God and saying:

> *Glory to God in the highest,*
> *And on earth peace, goodwill toward men"*
> Luke 2:13-14 (NKJV)[11]

Suddenly. The people had waited so long and now He was here. Many of them missed the miracle of His birth and life. Many weren't ready to accept that the answer had finally—suddenly—come.

We do the same thing. We wait and wait and somewhere inside we begin to doubt that He's going to answer. So, we stop looking. We stop anticipating. And when the answer comes, we're surprised. If we could look at our lives from above, we would probably see lots of events that gave lots of clues that "suddenly" was coming. But we can't. So, we miss out on the answers.

I'd love to say I don't live this way. After my experience all those years ago, you'd think I'd never be surprised by His "suddenly" again. But sadly, I am. And I am sure there have been many answers I've missed because I wasn't ready for "suddenly."

I want to do better. I pray that God will give me eyes to see and ears to hear. I ask that He help me commit to living in anticipation of the "suddenly," so I will be ready to say "yes" when "suddenly" comes.

Dangerous Prayers

"Call to me and I will answer you, and will tell you great and hidden things that you have not known." Jeremiah 33:3 (ESV)

Since mankind started praying, we have been praying dangerous prayers. David Livingstone, an incredible missionary and man of God, once prayed:

> *Send me anywhere, only go with me. Lay any burden on me, only sustain me. Sever any ties but the tie that binds me to Your service and to Your heart.*[12]

And God did. It was a pretty dangerous prayer. He died in what is present-day Zambia.

Not all our dangerous prayers will lead us to mission fields and foreign lands. They will, however, always change our lives in unexpected ways.

I prayed one of those dangerous prayers years ago. I knew when I uttered the words that it was a pretty scary prayer. I just couldn't see where it was going to actually lead me.

One night, sitting on the steps of my front porch, I found myself thinking about my calling from God. Actually, I was wondering if I *had* a calling and if I did, what it might be.

So, I prayed my dangerous prayer:

Lord, I'll go anywhere and do anything if You'll just show me where and how.

I figured that this prayer would some day lead me to the place of service, fulfilling an as yet unidentified calling God would place on my life. Like many of us, I wondered if maybe I'd wind up somewhere on a mission field. And someday, I may still wind up doing exactly that. But that has not been God's first answer to my dangerous prayer.

In 2013, I met the man who would become my husband. I lived in South Carolina, he lived in Tennessee. During one of our "phone" dates, he said, "I really like you and I think you feel the same way. But you live in South Carolina and I live in Tennessee, and I'm not moving."

To which I replied, "I'm a person who puts down very deep roots. I've made my home here; my family is here. That being said, I've always believed it's more about who you're with than where you are. Home is about people, not a place."

Fast forward a little over a year, and I found myself married, living in Nashville. It wasn't an easy transition; I knew no one, he was traveling, I didn't have a job for the first five months. Money was very tight. I knew I was with the one God had given me in the place where we were supposed to be. That didn't make it any easier.

Then, in December of 2016, two years after I married and moved away from everything and everyone I knew, I found myself one morning sitting down and writing a Facebook post about a Christmas song written and sung by some pretty incredible friends. I finished the post, put it out there for all to see, then read it to my husband.

And I found my calling. I haven't stopped writing since that morning. My husband keeps having these visions about where this is going to take me. A lot of that scares me. A lot of it I can't imagine happening.

But one morning while he and I were talking about all of this, my journey and my writing, God spoke. He reminded me of that front porch prayer. He reminded me of my commitment to Him, to go anywhere and do anything. And He said, "Here you are."

It's not where I thought I'd be. It's certainly not what I thought I'd be doing. But that's God. His ways are not our ways. His plans are seldom, if ever, our plans. We have ideas and plans and dreams. God promises that if we yield to Him, to His ways, we will live far beyond our wildest imaginations.

"Now to Him Who is able to do immeasurably more than all we ask or imagine, according to His power that is in work in us." Ephesians 3:20 (NIV)

It's scary to yield, to pray radical, dangerous prayers. We may find ourselves far from home, far from comfort, far from familiar.

But what we won't find ourselves is far from God. And we may just find ourselves living an adventure we never saw coming.

"Whether you turn to the right or the left, your ears will hear a voice behind you saying, 'This is the way, walk in it.'" Isaiah 30:21 (NIV)

If you haven't prayed one of those dangerous prayers, do it. Ask God to take you out of your comfort zone, away from the familiar, into a place you, right now, can't imagine. Give God a chance to show you how He can use you in answer to your dangerous prayer.

And see where you go. It'll be scary. It'll be challenging. And it'll be the adventure of a lifetime.

The Oxygen Mask

After He had sent the crowds away, He went up on the mountain by Himself to pray, and when it was evening, He was there alone. Matthew 14:23 (NASB)

A while back, I heard my husband talking with a minister friend who was going through a particularly hard time. He told him, "On a plane, when the attendants go over the emergency procedures, you are always told to put the oxygen mask on yourself before you help someone else. You'll be no help to yourself or anyone else if you don't take care of yourself first."

He went on to explain that this principal is true in ministry—and in life. If we're always running around taking care of others and never taking time for ourselves, we're soon running on empty and we're useless to everyone.

As Christians, we've somehow become convinced that taking care of ourselves is wrong, selfish. But that couldn't be further from the truth.

Jesus slipped away, or just got up and left and went to be alone with His Father. He needed time to refuel, regroup, refocus. And if the Son of God needed "me" time, I'm pretty sure we do, too.

I find it very difficult, even now, at times to pray for my needs and wants. Satan pokes at me, chastising me for my selfishness. But the Bible makes it clear that we are to bring our requests to God. There's nothing wrong with asking others to pray for you—the Bible encourages it. But Scripture calls—commands—us to also pray for our own needs and wants.

In Luke 18:1-8 (NIV), Jesus tells us the story of the persistent widow, ending it with *"And will not God bring about justice for His chosen ones, who cry out to Him day and night? Will He keep putting him off? I tell you, He will see that they get justice and quickly."*

Luke 11: 9-13 (NIV) exhorts us: *"So, I say to you: 'Ask and it will be given to you; seek and you will find; knock and the door will be opened to you. For everyone who asks receives; the one who seeks finds; and to the one who knocks, the door will be opened. Which of you fathers, if your son asks for a fish, will give him a snake instead? Or if he asks for an egg, will give him a scorpion? If you then, though you are evil, know how to give good gifts to your children, how much more will your Father in Heaven give the Holy Spirit to those who ask Him!'"*

I've come to realize a few things about praying for myself:

1. It's commanded in scripture.
2. If you want others to believe God hears and answers prayers, you better have some personal experience with what you're telling them.
3. Nothing grows our faith and strengthens our walk like seeing God work and answer prayers in our lives.
4. The more something matters, the more personally invested we are. And if we're personally invested, we will put our time and our prayers into it.
5. We gain great authority and confidence as we see God move in our lives because of our prayers.

So, yes, pray for others—never stop praying for others. But don't ever, ever stop praying for yourself. Give God the chance to show you—and everyone else who's watching—just how big He is.

Then step out to help others, lift them up, pray for them.

Just be sure to put the oxygen mask on yourself first.

One Of Ten

"One of them, when he saw he was healed, came back, praising God in a loud voice. He threw himself at Jesus' feet and thanked Him." Luke 17:15-16 (NIV)

In Luke 17: 11-19, we read about ten lepers who cried out to Jesus for healing. When Jesus saw them, He told them to go show themselves to the priest, who could declare them to be clean. They took off and on the way, they were healed.

One of the ten turned around and ran back to Jesus, threw himself at His feet, sobbing I'm sure, and thanked Him.

One came back. The other nine, although I am sure they were grateful, didn't even pause to thank Jesus for what He had done.

I'd like to say that I am always the one who came back. I'd even like to say that I'm *usually* the one who came back. But the reality is I am usually one of the nine.

Psalm 92:1 (NLT) says it is good to give thanks to the Lord.

Jesus constantly gave thanks before miracles happened: before He fed a crowd of over 5,000; before he fed 4,000; before He raised Lazarus from the dead.

The Bible is full of thanksgiving. We're instructed to bring our anxieties to the Lord with thanksgiving (Philippians 4:6 NIV).

But I don't. At least, not much. And when I do, there's often a caveat attached: "Thank You, but could You do this now?"

I really am one of the nine.

I don't want to be. I want to be filled with a heart and mind of gratitude, instead of being filled with thoughts that what He's done isn't enough.

I think that all of us, somewhere inside, wish we were more thankful. We know, on any given day, that we have been truly and wonderfully blessed. Just getting up each morning to face a new day should fill us with joy.

"This is the day the Lord has made. We will rejoice and be glad in in," declares Psalm 118:24 (NLT).

But do we? Do we wake up and rejoice and praise God? Do we open our eyes and thank God for the day, for our families, for His provisions before we start our day?

Or do we wake up to the flood of worries and problems that will meet us that day?

We know Philippians 4:6 (NIV) says, *"Do not be anxious about anything but in every situation, by prayer and petitions, with thanksgiving, present your request to God."*

So, we wake up, and yes, we can be bombarded by the worries and anxieties of the day. How we chose to move forward is up to us. We can bring our requests, our petitions, to the Lord. In fact, we're instructed to do just that. Start your day by discussing your day with God.

But don't stop there. Thank Him. I don't care how small the thanks are. I've been in that place, more than I care to recall, when finding *anything* to be thankful for felt impossible.

And then a bird would begin to sing and I would be reminded that He loves me more than the little birds. And I thank Him.

On those miserably muggy Southern summer mornings, a gentle breeze brushes my face. And I thank Him.

Small things in the overall scheme of what I'm facing, but God's love notes are everywhere. We just have to see them and thank the One who sent them.

You see what you look for.

What do we look for? If we start, or end, our days with the burdens, the troubles, the hurts of our lives, then everything else is colored by the grey blah of our thoughts. Everything we experience is dulled by the weight of our burdens.

But if we start, or end, our days with praise, with whatever, big or small, that brings us joy and gratitude, we will begin to see with eyes of gratitude. And everything we experience will be brightened by the lifting of the clouds.

Don't get me wrong. Changing our attitude, living with a grateful heart, doesn't necessarily change our circumstances. But it certainly changes our perspective.

Look again at the ten lepers. All cleaned. Nine of them were, I suspect, immediately focused on how this would change things, how they could go back to their families and resume their lives. Their focus was entirely on themselves and their new lease on life.

But for one leper, his focus was not on himself but on the One who gave him the new lease on life. And rather than focus just on what he had gotten, he decided to focus on the One who gave it to him.

The men had a decision to make. Only one chose gratitude.

Each of us have the same choices. Each of us can focus on what's wrong or we can focus on the One Who can make it right.

Paul said we are to fix our eyes on Jesus. (Hebrews 12:2, NIV)

The old hymn says, "Turn your eyes toward Jesus. Look full in His wonderful face. And the things of earth will grow strangely dim in the light of His glory and grace."[13]

Our world is always going to hold troubles, pain and hurt. Jesus actually assured us that it would: *"In this world you will have trouble."* But look at the whole verse: *"I have told you these things so that in Me you may have peace. In this world, you will have trouble. But take heart! I have overcome the world."* John 16:33 (NIV)

And the verse in Philippians that tells us to pray with thanksgiving is followed by yet another promise: *"And the peace of God, which surpasses all understanding, will guard your hearts and minds in Christ Jesus."* Philippians 4:7 (ESV)

The choice is ours. Do we focus on ourselves, on our problems? Are we one of the nine?

Or do we focus on each gift, each blessing? Do we focus on the Giver? Do we turn our eyes off ourselves and onto Jesus?

Are we one of ten who remembers to say, "Thank you."?

What Faith Is Not

"When I am afraid, I put my trust in You." Psalm 56:3 (NIV)

We've gone through some really tough times. When we were first married, my husband's job situation was highly stressful. Eventually, he became unemployed. We've struggled. A lot. We've prayed. A lot. As we went through those long months, waiting for God to move and answer our prayers, people would come to us to tell us that we were great witnesses to them. Others have told us how they've been watching us and how our faith has inspired and encouraged them.

Their words bless me. They humble me. And they shame me.

They bless me because I know our struggles have had a purpose. I'm blessed because God is using and has used us to somehow reach and help others. God's Word says that *"God causes everything to work together for the good of those who love God and are called according to His purpose for them."* Romans 8:28 (NLT)

The struggles we have faced, and are still facing, are working together for our good—even when we can't always see how—and for the good of those who are watching us. We have been called according to His purpose. I feel as if we're soldiers in a war, serving at the pleasure of our Leader and our Lord. It is an honor to serve him, to be used for His purpose and His glory.

I'm humbled because God is using us. I am most certainly not the best choice He could have made to be this kind of witness. I know I have limitations and failings and yet these people have seen something in me, in us, that helps them. I'm humbled as I've watch my husband move forward each day, working as unto the Lord to accomplish and fulfill the vision God has laid on his heart. I am humbled by those who have come alongside us, at our lowest points, sent by God to uplift and encourage us.

I'm humbled by the amazing ways God has provided for us, the calls and texts, the prayers, the gifts. God has richly blessed us through these struggles and His great love and provision humbles me.

And I'm shamed. I have walked with the Lord for a lot of years. I've seen miracle after miracle in my life and in the lives of so many others. And yet I doubt. I fear. I panic. It's as if I start all over every time the struggle gets too hard, when the future is totally unknown. Rather than trusting, rather than remembering all the times He has come through and provided for us, rather than clinging to His promises, I panic. I get horribly impatient with Him and I am overwhelmed by fear.

We hear pastors and well-meaning believers tell us that faith and fear can't live with each other. That you can't have faith if you have fear, and you can't have fear if you have faith.

But through this journey, I have come to realize, in my life, a very important truth:

Faith isn't the absence of fear. Faith is moving forward in the midst of the fear. It's trusting in the One who conquered death and the grave. It's looking fear in the eye and saying, "Do you worst. My God is always going to be bigger than my fear."

The Bible says, *"Perfect love (the love of Christ) casts out fear."* I John 4:18 (ESV; note added)

For me, this is a continual casting out. When I was a teen, I struggled with unexplainable, undeniable fear. I had a plaque on my wall of I John 4:18. I'd wake in the middle of the night, terrified for no discernible reason, and I'd stare through the darkness to where the poster hung, and I'd repeat those words over and over: "Perfect love casts out fear; perfect love casts out fear; perfect love casts out fear." Eventually God's peace would again fill me, and I'd go back to sleep.

The fear has never really left me. It comes in all kinds of ways: Will those I love safely arrive home? Will my bills be paid? Will illness take someone close to me?

Rational or not, the fear is real. And Satan, who is the author of the fear, has a heyday with me. He beats me up with doubts about the strength of my faith; he taunts me that this just might be the time God doesn't come through; he reminds me of every heartbreak and disappointment in my past, when God didn't seem present and His purpose was—or still is—unclear.

And I get angry at myself. I feel I should do better, be better. With all the blessings and miracles I've witnessed, how can I still fear?

Sound familiar?

So, I'm shamed when I hear that I'm a witness to others, a blessing in their lives.

But then I am reminded that this—the witness, the blessing—is not about me; it's about God. It's not about the one who prays and tries to believe and trust; it's about the One to whom we pray, the One in whom we believe, the One we trust.

We are—I am—a work in progress.

My journey has miles to go. And every day I pray and every time I confess, "Lord, I believe; help my unbelief." He draws me closer; my faith gets bigger and my fear gets smaller.

Jesus told us that if we have the faith of a mustard seed, we can move mountains. I'm not sure some days if my faith is even that big. But it's getting there. It isn't perfect. Fear still stains it. But God specializes in using we fearful, faithful people to bless and encourage a world of other fearful, faithful folks.

In Zechariah 4:10 (NLT), it talks about not being ashamed of small beginnings. My faith has had a small beginning.

God can and has used even my small beginning to help and encourage others. And that helps and encourages me. God can and does use the smallest things for His glory:

A sling and three pebbles

A couple of fish and five loaves of bread

A baby born in a manger

So, He'll use my faith, no matter how small and battered by fear, for His glory. Maybe fear-battered faith is a blessing. Maybe believing in spite of the fear is the miracle.

Maybe the fear never entirely goes away. I hope it does. I'd love to trust and never doubt. Until that day, I'll keep trusting through the doubt and my faith, each day, will grow bigger than my fear.

And God will get all the glory.

Through It All

"Peace I leave with you; My peace I give you. I do not give to you as the world gives. Do not let your heart be troubled and do not be afraid." John 14:27 (NIV)

"Do not let your heart be troubled and do not be afraid." How I wish it were that simple—Jesus commanded it; I should be able to obey.

And some days I can. Some days I rise on wings of an eagle and soar above all the trials and problems of life. But, some days—most days, if I'm honest—I'm not soaring. I'm bogged down in my fears, my worries, my anxieties. I don't want to be. But here I am, again.

It's been said there are 365 versions of "fear not" or "don't be afraid" in the Bible, one for every day of the year. God obviously knows we're going to struggle with our fears and doubts as long as we're walking this earth. We wonder at times why God allows circumstances in our lives that can fill us with fear, worry and anxiety. We don't understand His reasoning or His purpose.

There's an old southern gospel song entitled "Through it All." The last verse says:

"For if I'd never had a problem,
I wouldn't know God could solve them
I wouldn't know what faith in God could do."[14]

Our strongest earthly relationships are with those who have stood by us, who have proven they are on our side, that they will stand up for us when needed. They have proven their love and commitment to us. We know we matter to them.

It's the same with God. Through the trials and heartaches of our lives, He has stood by us, He has fought for us, He has defended us. He has proven to be faithful. He doesn't run away from our fear and worry; He walks with us through them.

I remember years ago talking to my pastor about Daddy. I told him Daddy had the strongest faith of anyone in my life and I wished mine was as solid as his. This wise pastor told me Daddy's faith didn't just pop up one day, fully grown; his faith had become what it was because of all the years of walking with God and watching Him prove His faithfulness over and over. After a lifetime of walking with God and trusting Him, Daddy knew He could be trusted.

I wish I could say I have that kind of faith. I'm not there—yet. I still worry and fear. And God understands. He never walks away. Through it all, He keeps showing me He is faithful, that He cares. Each time I see—eventually—through my fears and worries that He is faithful to help me overcome the fear and worry and I again trust that He will carry me through.

"I have told you these things so that in Me you may have peace. In this world, you will have trouble. But take heart! I have overcome the world." John 16:33 (NIV)

A Beautiful Mess

"See, I am doing a new thing! Now it springs up; do you not perceive it? I am making a way in the wilderness and streams in the wasteland." Isaiah 43:19 (NIV)

Most of us have times when we'd like to hit the "reset" button, erase everything and start over. We think that we would do life better if we could go back—or move forward—without all the messes we've accumulated.

But the truth is, every mess, mistake, heartache, victory, and joy has led us to who we are today. All of us are the sum total of our life experiences.

Each of us is a beautiful mess. We live in a fallen world; we have, on many occasions, fallen ourselves. We carry with us all that we are and have been. And God promises that He will use it all to make a new thing. Not a new thing with no past or baggage, but a new thing that comes *out of* our past and baggage. He takes all that we are and creates a new thing, reshaping it into something beautiful, a "way in the wilderness and streams in the wasteland."

Most days, I'm not sure I can find my way out of the wilderness, the wasteland. All I see are my mistakes and sins. I can't see past my present to a future where God can use me for good. But one of the wonderful things about God is that when I ask Him for forgiveness for all my failures and mistakes, He graciously grants it.

We all struggle with letting go of the our past; we can't imagine that God can actually forget our sins and use our lives for any good.

But Hebrews 8:12 (NIV) promises that He does just that: *"Now I will forgive their wickedness and will remember their sins no more."*

And Psalm 103:12 (NIV) assures us, *"As far as the east is from the west, so far has He removed our transgressions from us."*

Even though the scars and baggage of our past weigh us down, He promises that He will create a new thing within us.

"Therefore, if anyone is in Christ, he is a new creation. The old has passed away; behold the new is come." II Corinthians 5:17 (ESV)

So, we come to Him with our baggage and messes. We ask Him to take this bundle of life's stuff and turn it into something new and good. We ask Him to use all that has made us who we are to create a "new thing" in us. And we move into the new with hope and anticipation, eagerly waiting to see how our loving Father will make us into new creations.

Red Sea Moments

"The Lord will fight for you; you need only be still." Exodus 14:14 (NIV)

"I would have despaired unless I had believed that I would see the goodness of the Lord in the land of the living." Psalm 27:13 (NASB)

When we read the story of Moses leading the Israelites out of Egypt, it's easy for us to roll our eyes at their fear and lack of faith. God had rescued them from Pharaoh, led them out of Egypt and straight to the Red Sea. And Pharaoh decided he wanted them back and was hot on their trail with his whole army.

Even if Pharaoh hadn't shown up, there was still the sea to cross and no boats in sight. The Israelites panicked. They began to grumble. And we, reading their story, shake our heads at their lack of faith.

But they didn't know how the story ended. We do.

It's easy to be judgey and condemning on this side of the miracle. But aren't we just like the Israelites? We start out on our journey, full of confidence, sure God is with us.

Then we hit a roadblock. And it may be huge, Red Sea huge and we start to fear. We start to hear rumblings of the enemy coming up behind us and the worry turns into full-blown panic. We start questioning our decisions to step out in faith; we start questioning God. Maybe we heard Him wrong; maybe we made a really, really bad move when we started this journey.

I think most believers who have accomplished great things for God would confess that they have had Red Sea moments—days, weeks, months—when they were all but paralyzed by fear, questioning if they had truly heard from God or if God had changed His mind and walked away.

But Deuteronomy 31:8 (NIV) promises: *"It is the Lord who goes before you. He will be with you; He will not leave you or forsake you. Do not fear or be dismayed."*

When we decide to move in and toward our calling in Christ, we will all have Red Sea moments when the sea is before us and the enemy is closing in on us. We will be tempted to panic. We may very well panic. But we *cannot* allow panic to win. We have to stand and remember that the God who brought us to the sea will lead us through the sea. We have to face that water, knowing our God is big enough to part it or completely dry it up. We keep moving, through the fear, to victory on the other side.

There will come a time when we are on the other side of the miracle, when we see all He has done to lead us and protect us and provide for us. We will rejoice in our victory, knowing it is truly God's victory.

But while you are in your Red Sea moment, remember there is a miracle waiting to happen. If it happened for those complaining, doubting Israelites, it will happen for us. Hold onto God's promises. Hold onto who you *know* Him to be. Face the obstacle and remind yourself that God is always, always bigger.

Command the Red Sea to part in Jesus' name. Then, cross over on dry land to the other side of your miracle.

This New Country

"Leave your country and your people. Leave your father's family and go to the country that I will show you." Genesis 12:1 (ERV)[15]

My married life, while incredible, is nothing like I thought it would be, a statement which I am sure is echoed by every spouse everywhere. We all go into marriage with at least some vague idea of what to expect. We are, if we're honest, almost always wrong.

Having never lived more than 90 minutes from my family, I realized that moving over eight hours away would require huge logistical adjustments. No more jumping in the car and heading home on a whim. No more meeting halfway and picking up little ones for the weekend. I left behind a great job and awesome friends.

Until you've experienced it, no one can explain the shock of walking away from everything that makes you who you are, arriving at a new, unknown place, and looking around at this alien landscape that is now your new home. Many, those wonderfully adventurous, extroverted souls, embrace the new with great delight and enthusiasm. The rest of us, the deeply rooted, settled introverts, do not.

To say that this was not what I anticipated would be a vast understatement. I think I understand a little of how Abraham must have felt. Here he was, settled with his wife and relatives, 75 years old. And God speaks to him and tells him to get up and leave everything and everyone he knows.

There were days where I felt that, like Abraham, God had led me to this "country that I will show you," but instead of hanging around and explaining why I was here, He sat me down and said, "I'll be right back," and left! It was scary, unfamiliar, and very lonely.

But in this foreign land, full of challenges, fear, love, and discovery, I found the greatest of all surprises.

Me.

When there are no distractions, when all you see are detours you never expected, leading you down roads you never planned to travel, all pretense gets stripped away. You become, for better or worse, your most true self.

I'd be the first to admit that there were, at least at first, much more "worse" than "better." Like many of us, my default emotion is fear and lots of it. I spent many hours praying to, pleading with, and yelling at God. I have discovered, in my deepest, rawest place, that there is apparently nothing I can say or scream at God that will cause Him to walk away.

In the short time I've been in this marriage with which God has graced me, I find that I am becoming my most true self. I know, in this short time, more about myself, my husband, and most importantly, my God than I ever imagined possible. I have found, after all these years, who I am meant to be. I am beginning my journey to get to know the real me.

God has stripped away every idea I had about who I am, what marriage looks like, and who a husband should be. He has anointed me with blessings and He has gifted me with the perfect man for my journey. I loved him when I married him. I adore him more and more each day.

My husband has prodded and pushed and encouraged me to find my voice. He has showered me with words of affirmation and support. No one has ever loved me the way he does. He listens when I share this new vision God has given me. He holds me when it becomes too much.

God did not, of course, leave me alone in this new country. He did lead me, as David wrote, beside still waters. He restored my soul. (Psalm 23: 2-3, ESV)

We all, at various times, find ourselves in that new country. We may not like the journey. We may not want to be at the destination. But God has a plan and a purpose. We just have to yield to His call and head in the direction in which He's leading. It's scary. But He promises He will never leave nor forsake us (Deuteronomy 31:6, NIV).

I'm glad God doesn't grant us the ability to see into the future. Most of us would be too scared to take those first steps.

And we would miss out on all the blessings and discoveries He has for us in that new country.

Our Hero

"For we do not have a High Priest who is unable to empathize with our weaknesses, but we have One who has been tempted in every way, just as we are—yet He did not sin. Let us then approach God's throne of grace with confidence, so that we may receive mercy and find grace to help us in our time of need." Hebrews 4:15-16 (NIV)

Recently, God revealed to me that, while I was praying and praising God for His yet unseen answers and miraculous provision, deep within my heart were doubts that He ever intended to answer my prayers.

It was a rather humbling, embarrassing moment. I was stunned to realize exactly how much doubt festered inside of me.

As Christians, we are told to pray and believe and never doubt. So, we pray and praise, and say we believe. But somewhere deep inside, at least in my case, is deep-seeded doubt. At times, late at night or when the discouragement and fear come close to overwhelming, I catch a quick glimmer of the doubt before I turn away, not acknowledging its presence, always attempting to be that faithful, undoubting Christian.

That night, I ran head-first into the doubt, caught off guard and unable to deflect or avoid it. I realized in that moment that this was a giant barrier in my walk and relationship with God. My failure to acknowledge this doubt and confess it left a huge lie between the Father and me. My heart actually hurt when I realized how long I had harbored this unbelief and doubt. As I confessed and asked for forgiveness, God graciously forgave me (I imagine a bit relieved that I had finally caught on), and opened a door deep in my spirit, revealing a great, vitally important truth: Satan really, really hates us.

This is, of course, no great surprise. Scripture warns us, over and over, of Satan's hate and deep desire to destroy us.

I Peter 5:8 (ESV) tells us, *"Be sober-minded, be watchful. Your adversary the devil prowls around like a roaring lion seeking someone to devour."*

Devour. What a powerful word. Not just harm; he wants to totally destroy us, annihilate us. Satan will do anything—anything—to keep God's children from victory and joy. He can't keep us out of Heaven, he can't touch our eternity, but he will certainly do everything he can to destroy our lives here on earth.

For generations, he has made sure that the message we receive about him is diluted, that in our minds, we have decided that he is an almost irrelevant figure. No more the hellfire and brimstone, pulpit-pounding sermons that warn us to flee from Satan, that show him to be a very real, very present threat. We've come to believe that talking about or thinking about Satan makes us weird, out of step, or hyper-spiritual. So, we instead focus our attention on God, which is of course we should, ignoring the prince of darkness, the ruler of this world.

Satan has whispered to us, in that sly, condescending voice of his, that we really are not that important to him. He chastises us for even considering that we warrant his attention when there are so many others doing so much more for the Kingdom. He feeds our sense of failure as Christians, reminding us of what a small, small part we play in God's plan.

So, we believe the lie. We know—the Bible tells us—that Satan is our enemy, but we no longer associate the trials, struggles and heartaches of our lives to him. After all, he's too busy to waste his time on us.

And then Satan takes it a step further. The lie becomes more dark and dangerous. If we are too insignificant to matter to Satan, why on earth would we matter to God? If all the pain, suffering and trouble we go through doesn't come from Satan—since he can't be bothered with us—then someone else has to be responsible. And that someone has to be God.

Of course, God doesn't directly harm us—we aren't that important to Him. He just simply isn't stepping in to stop it.

And now Satan has us right where he wants us. Sure he's not after us and sure God's not for us.

In *Captivating*, by Staci and John Elredge, she makes an incredibly profound statement: "You are passionately loved by the God of the universe. You are passionately hated by his enemy."[16]

Passionately hated by God's enemy. We're never taught that. We hear about sin, we hear about redemption, about resisting temptation, about the power of prayer. We hear about the power of God's love. We never hear about the power of Satan's hatred.

Scripture is full of warnings about Satan. If God takes Satan so seriously, shouldn't we?

The most successful generals win wars by knowing their enemy. Championship sports teams spend countless hours poring over videos of their opponents, learning their weaknesses and strengths. We have been given the Word of God, the ultimate weapon to overcome our enemy. And unlike generals and athletes, we have a guarantee of victory.

We are called to be aware. If you don't know there's an enemy, you'll always be surprised by his attacks. God has provided all we need to overcome and defeat our most dangerous foe. And He's promised He will always be there with us, fighting for us to ensure we win. (Romans 8:37)

Being aware that we have an enemy is part of the battle. The bigger part is knowing what to do. James exhorts us,

"Submit yourselves, then, to God. Resist the devil, and he will flee from you." James 4:7 (NIV)

We certainly can't do that on our own. God has promised He will give us strength to overcome. He's also promised He is fighting for us and with us.

Hebrews 4:15-16 (NIV) gives us two important truths: 1) we have a High Priest, Jesus, who understands the temptations Satan throws at us; and 2) we are invited to enter right into the Throne Room with our needs and requests, promised mercy and grace in our time of need.

Our Champion in this war with the enemy is Jesus. He was tempted by Satan, aced all the same temptations we face, and didn't sin. He certainly understands Satan's schemes and what we face, and He's our means of escape.

Jesus is our great protector. When Satan comes after us—and he will, over and over—we must be able to recognize the attack and immediately turn to our Warrior Savior for our defense.

My Daddy was an incredibly Godly, faithful man, very quiet and non-confrontational. He strongly believed that everyone should try to get along and live in peace and he practiced that philosophy in his own life every day. But, let someone come after one of his children and he became a totally different person, a mighty warrior defending the ones he loved. I never doubted that my Daddy would defend and protect me. He was always my defender, he was always my hero.

God does the same thing for us. He defends us. He is with us in every one of our enemy's attacks. No matter how loud the enemy or how fierce his attacks, God stands with us and for us and we need never fear or doubt.

He is our Hero.

"So do not fear, for I am with you; do not be dismayed, for I am your God. I will strengthen you and help you; I will uphold you with My righteous right hand." Isaiah 41:10 (NIV)

Fishes And Loaves

"Another of His disciples, Andrew, Simon Peter's brother, spoke up, 'Here is a boy with five small barley loaves and two small fish, but how far will they go among so many?'" John 6:8-9 (NIV)

John 6: 1-13 is the story of the miracle of the fishes and loaves. I've read this story, heard sermons preached about it, many times. Jesus took five loaves and two fish, blessed them, and fed over 5,000 men, women and children. It is, as miracles go, a pretty big, public one.

But recently, as I read this passage, I saw it with very different eyes.

Jesus asked Philip how he thought the crowd could be fed. Philip, seeing with earthly eyes, immediately explained why it couldn't happen.

Philip answered him, "It would take more than half a year's wages to buy enough bread for each one to have a bite!" John 6:7 (NIV)

I do this. We all do. Problems arise, crises come, and our first response is to focus on the problem. We're all a bit like Philip.

Then there's Andrew. Jesus wasn't even talking to him but he answered anyway—'Here's a child with five loaves and two fish. Can You do anything with this?'

Sort of a silly question, isn't it?

Five thousand plus hungry people.

A little boy's snack.

In Matthew 18:3, Jesus tells us we have to have faith as a little child to come to Him.

And here's a little boy, who brings his meal and somehow never doubts it can be used.

And then there's Andrew. He'd seen the water turned into wine. He'd seen the lame man jump up and run. So, he comes, bringing a little boy and a small meal, and asks,

"It's not much. Can you do anything with this?"

And Jesus takes what's offered and says, "Well, let's see. Hand it over and I'll take it from here."

And boy, does He!

I want to be that little boy. I want to be Andrew. I want to bring my life, my talents to Jesus, with the faith of a little child, and hand it to Him.

"It's not much. Can You do anything with this?"

And I want to see what He'll do.

Maybe He uses me to feel thousands. Maybe he breaks me, blesses me, and uses me in ways I can't begin to imagine. I don't know how He'll use my yielded life.

Here's what I do know:

- I have to come with the faith of a child, never doubting He can do what needs to be done.
- I have to give myself and all that I have to Him.
- Jesus will take all I give Him and make it into so much more.
- Others will be blessed.
- Blessings will overflow.

The Scriptures tell us that when everyone had enough to eat, they gathered up the leftovers—12 baskets full.

One basket for each disciple, so each of them could personally touch and see the abundance of God's provisions.

Ephesians 3:20 (NIV) promises us God is always able to do immeasurably more than we can ask or imagine.

So, bring your "fishes and loaves" to Him. And watch how He'll use it to abundantly bless.

Mama's Pound Cake

"Don't try to get out of anything prematurely. Let it do its work so you become mature and well developed." James 1:4 (MSG)

I have, on more than one occasion, informed the Lord that I am perfectly content with my maturity and Christian development. I have declared that my character and faith are deep enough, even if they have the depth of a mud puddle. I do not need—and certainly do not want—another trial or another learning experience.

Odd as it may be, God has not, not once, agreed with me. He doesn't take me out of the struggle, the hardship, and the pain.

He takes me through it.

James tells us we are not to try to get out of anything prematurely. Instead, we're to let the situation, the trial, the heartaches do their work so we can become "mature and well developed."

Apparently, this is a big deal to God. And, if I'm honest, He's right (I know, big shocker). On the other side, sometimes, even in the middle of, those places I don't want to be, I realize I'm learning and growing.

In Habakkuk 2:3, God declares, *"These things I plan won't happen right away. Slowly, steadily, surely, the time approaches when the vision will be fulfilled. If it seems slow, do not despair, for these things will surely come to pass. Just be patient! They will not be overdue a single day!"* (TLB)[17]

No matter how many times I go through one of these times of waiting, I find there is still a part of me that's afraid that this will be the time God won't come through, that the answers will be overdue.

Many times, more times than I care to admit, I've tried to help God along and get a quicker answer.

It never ends well.

My Mama was an incredible cook. Our favorite creations were, no surprise, her desserts. She made the best cakes. And one of her specialties was her pound cake.

Pound cakes are great culinary creations, not just because of their mouth-watering flavor and light, airy texture, but because of what's involved in creating them. From start to finish, it takes about an hour to put together. There's lots of egg cracking, butter melting, flour sifting and ingredient mixing. The cake pan must be prepared just so. After all the preparation, the batter is poured, and the cake goes in the oven to bake.

And bake. Ninety long, excruciating minutes. The scent fills the house; your taste buds dance in anticipation, for what seems like forever. Habakkuk 2:3 could have been written for just this time.

Pound cakes are very temperamental creations and, if not treated with care, will, to the great dismay and frustration of the baker, "fall." Footsteps must be light, voices soft. And no matter what, the oven door is not to be opened until every single one of those 90 minutes has passed.

If done right, the cake will emerge from the oven—finally—tall, airy and melt-in-your-mouth delicious.

If, however, you try to rush the process, if you don't trust the instructions and open the oven door—you know, just in case the recipe was wrong and it finished before its time—that beautiful masterpiece that had risen, brown and perfect, will begin, right in front of your eyes, to shrink down into the pan like a water-logged sponge left out in the sun. Your beautiful creation is no more.

Don't get me wrong; it's still good. It's just not what it could have been.

It's the same with us. God has a plan—a vision—for us, one He knows we can only receive by going through the waiting, for only in the waiting do we become able to receive the answer. We can rush things and try to move God along to get us out and to an earlier resolution. And sometimes, we get a resolution of sorts. It may be good. After all, God promises He will work all things together for our good (Romans 8:28 NLT). It just may not be the best.

I want God's best. I'm learning, much to my dismay, that I am usually the reason I don't always get it. I try to rush Him, I try to get ahead and help Him get me to where He wants me to be.

I open the oven door.

In her later years, Mama almost never baked. But since she's been gone, my brother has picked up the torch and is carrying on her baking legacy. He has conquered her pound cake recipe and creates a masterpiece that would make her proud. Now that he's the baker, we understand even more what's involved in getting to the vision of that cake. And we appreciate it even more.

So, as I wait, I will try to remember His promises. I will try to go through the trials and lessons with great anticipation of what's coming on the other side. I will try to trust that the time for the answer is coming, that it will not be late, but instead right on time. And I will, hopefully, resist the urge to try to help Him along the way.

And maybe, I'll learn to not open the oven door.

"Yet what we suffer now is nothing compared to the glory He will reveal to us later." Romans 8:18 (NLT)

Glory To Glory

"And we all, with unveiled face, beholding as in a mirror the glory of the Lord, are being transformed into the same image, **from glory to glory***, even as from the Lord, the Spirit."* (II Corinthians 3:18 (NASB, emphasis added)

I have a friend who says the toughest place for a Christian to be is in the "to." As we grow as believers, there are mountaintop moments, when we feel as if we're standing right up there with God. But we never get to stay there.

I remember as a kid being told, "God loves you just as you are, but He loves you too much to leave you there."

Glory to glory.

I've spent a lot of time in the "to." There have been moments when I've sat with Jesus, His arm around me as He whispered words of love and assurance. There have been times I felt I was standing boldly in the throne room, Jesus at my side, as I presented my requests directly to the Father. There have been beautiful visits by the Holy Spirit when I have been totally overwhelmed by the love that filled and surrounded me.

But there have been many, many days and weeks and months of silence, times when, even though I knew God was listening, I felt ignored. And while I would like to think my faith has grown, there have been way too many days of doubt and unbelief.

Living in the "to."

Most of this is, I am sure, of my own making. I find myself thinking about how far I haven't come. I struggle with wanting the miracles for which I've prayed and with wondering what I'm doing or not doing that keeps them from coming, or even if my shortcomings and failings have anything to do with it.

God's Word promises that He is working all things for our good. I believe that. I just wonder how long it's going to take to get me there.

The one thing I do know, even if I don't always like it, is that there is still so much I need to learn. So, I'll be here, in this "to," until God moves me to the next "glory." There will be times of mountaintop moments along the way. And hopefully, I'll get to stay a bit longer the next time I get there.

I don't want to miss anything He's teaching me. So, for now, I'll rejoice that He loves me enough to bring me to and through the "to," and that He never leaves me here alone or forever.

And I'll wait with great joy and anticipation for the next "glory."

My Morning Choice

"Be anxious for nothing, but in everything by prayer and supplication with thanksgiving let your requests be made known to God. And the peace of God that surpasses all comprehension will guard your hearts and minds in Christ Jesus." Philippians 4:6-7 (NASB)

Most mornings, I wake up and immediately face the anxiety trying to well up and overtake me. It's kind of a "good morning, here's your daily dose of worry," start to the day. For longer than I want to admit, I rolled right into the day shrouded in the anxiety and fear of the coming hours.

Finally, after a much too long battle, God got my attention. It was a challenge to tear my focus off the worries of the day and put my eyes back on Him. I knew the truth of Philippians 4:7, but like most of us, I didn't want peace; I wanted answers, pronto.

But that's not how God usually works. While I'm in the middle of all my mess, my trials, my dark, scary place, God promises peace. What He doesn't promise is a quick solution.

There are marvelous promises of God's provisions in His Word:

"Now all glory to God, who is able through His mighty power at work within us, to accomplish infinitely more than we might ask or think." Ephesians 3:20 (NLT)

"And my God will meet all your needs according to the riches of His glory in Christ Jesus." Philippians 4:19 (NIV)

"Their trust should be in God, who richly gives us all we need for our enjoyment." I Timothy 6:17 (NIV)

There are a lot of promises of provision and victory in God's Word. Not a one of them comes with a delivery date. My husband's favorite verse in the Bible is Galatians 6:9 (NASB):

"Let us not lose heart in doing good, for in due time we will reap if we do not grow weary."

So, while I'm waiting for His "due time," I fret, I fear, I grow anxious.

But, I have a choice. Every single morning before I open my eyes, I get to choose: anxious or joyful, fear or peace.

Some mornings, of course, it's harder than others. But, then I turn my heart and mind to Jesus. I fill my mind with songs of praise. And I again remind myself:

"What then shall we say in response to these things? If God is for us, who can be against us? He who did not spare His own Son but gave Him up for us all, how will He not also, along with Him, graciously give us all things?" Romans 8:31-32 (NIV)

He took care of the biggest need I'll ever have, my separation from Him. After that, what on earth should I be anxious about?

When I think about it that way, it seems sort of silly, sinful even, to fret about the day-to-day stuff. But I do. We do. Since Satan has lost us for eternity, his only recourse is to try to destroy our day-to-day peace.

We have to choose. Do we look to God or listen to Satan?

Our humanness cries out, during those early morning hours, for answers. God gently whispers, "Peace, be still. I've got this."

Satan screams that God doesn't care. Our choice, every day, sometimes every hour, is who gets our attention.

So, what do we choose? How do we start our day?

David was very aware of the anxieties of the day; he lived for years with the constant threat of death at the hands of Saul. He knew he had been anointed as the next king of Israel; he just didn't see how it was going to happen. He clung to God's promise with no delivery date in sight. And while he waited, he remembered the goodness and the deliverance of the Lord. David's words are for us today.

"But as for me, I will sing about Your power. Each morning I will sing with joy about Your unfailing love. For You have been my refuge, a place of safety, when I am in distress." Psalm 59: 16 (NLT)

Divine Appointments

"But as it is written: 'Eye has not seen, nor ear heard, nor have entered into the heart of man the things which God has prepared for those who love Him'". I Corinthians 2:9 (NKJV)

When we pray regularly, irregular things will happen.

Since I started having a consistent morning prayer and quiet time, there have certainly been some irregular things that have happened, both good and bad. And I suspect many irregular things have happened I didn't even recognize. God often works through and for us when we aren't even aware it's happening. My spiritual vision really needs adjusting.

I realize there are times when I am just going through the motions. I read, I pray, I write. But I don't walk away from the time filled with a holy anticipation of what the day will bring, of how the Holy Spirit will show up and show off. I don't walk into my day, dedicating it to the Lord or dedicating myself to His calling. I just say "amen" and go about my day.

No wonder there are no divine appointments to keep. I don't even check the calendar!

So, I'm asking God to change that. I'm asking Him to show up and show me what He wants me to do, how He wants me to do it and who He wants involved.

I want to start my day, saying as Isaiah did, *"Here I am. Send me!"* Isaiah 6:8 (NIV)

Most of the changes in my life have been, I fear, in spite of me and not because of me. God has certainly had His work cut out for Him. So, I ask and hope that I will be more yielded and more open to what He wants to change. I want the good work He began in me to move closer to completion. I pray that as I move forward, there will be such huge changes that all will be able to see that I have been in the presence of God. I want to draw men and women to Him.

There are miracles I daily pray will rain down upon us. I want to walk in His miracles and, more importantly, I want to *see* that I'm walking in His miracles. I pray that I will have eyes to see and ears to hear.

I wait, in great anticipation, to see what God has in store for and in me.

May I meet and keep all my divine appointments!

Take Him At His Word

"Let us hold fast the confession of our hope without wavering for He who promised is faithful." Hebrews 10:23 (ESV)

"When Jesus had called the twelve together, He gave them power and authority to drive out all demons and to cure diseases, and He sent them to proclaim the kingdom of God and to heal the sick . . . So, they went out and went from village to village, proclaiming the good news and healing people everywhere." Luke 9:1-2, 6 (NIV)

Leonard Ravenhill once said, "One of these days, some simple soul will pick up the Book of God, read it, and believe it. Then the rest of us will be embarrassed."[18]

I wonder what would happen if that "simple soul" was me. Or you. If we stopped listening to our past and our doubts and our fears and we just ***believed***.

We read the account in Luke and think, 'yeah, but they had Jesus. If He told me to go do stuff like that, I'd go. I'd proclaim the good news and heal people. Those guys had it easy. They had Jesus.'

Did they? Did they really have it easy? Remember, Jesus' ministry was pretty short lived. And the Twelve had only been observers up until this point. Now, Jesus is sending them out on their own. The training wheels are off the bike. He told them to go and off they went.

And it worked. They shared the good news of Jesus. They healed the sick.

Because Jesus told them to.

We don't know how long they were gone. We don't know what Jesus did while they were gone. We do know they came back and told Him all about what had transpired (verse 10).

When I was in college, my best friend's mother was a second mother to me. She was fun, wise, sassy, talented, and encouraging. She was also one of the Godliest people I have ever had the honor to know. If I had a need, a prayer request, I would immediately call Thelma. After I shared my burden with her, her reply was always the same. "I will take that to my Lord."

I always hung up the phone filled with peace, knowing that 1) Thelma was immediately on her knees interceding for me; and 2) she and I never doubted that God would answer.

This precious saint went Home to the Lord several years ago. I am confident she is a part of the "great cloud of witnesses," still interceding for me.

So, what would our world look like, what would we look like if we read the Bible and truly believed it?

"If you have faith as small as a mustard seed, you can say to this mount, 'Move from here to there' and it will move. Nothing will be impossible for you." Matthew 17:20 (NIV)

"You can ask for anything in my name, and I will do it, so that the Son may bring glory to the Father." John 14:13 (NLT)

"Never will I leave you, never will I forsake you." Hebrews 13:5b (NIV)

"For no matter how many promises God has made, they are all 'Yes' in Christ. And so, through Him, the 'Amen' is spoken by us to the glory of God." II Corinthians 1:20 (NIV)

Is the "amen" (which means "so be it") really spoken by us? When did we stop believing the Bible?

Most of you, when you read that question, will shake your heads and adamantly deny that it's true. Of course we believe the Bible! We're Christians!

But do we **live** like we believe? Do we pray for lost family members and friends and truly believe they'll repent and turn to Christ?

My nephews have a half-brother who had a very rough time growing up. He hated God, for some pretty legitimate reasons. I prayed, on and off, for years for his salvation. When he gave his heart to the Lord a few years ago, I was thrilled. And surprised. And then really convicted. I think I had prayed, hoping, but not really believing. I was humbled—and a bit shamed—that God had answered such a weak, doubting prayer.

What if we prayed, not just our requests, but our thanks for what He's doing and going to do. What if we claimed the truth of His promises and **acted** as if they were already fulfilled. Because, according to Scripture, they are.

"I will answer them before they even call to me. While they are still talking about their needs, I will go ahead and answer their prayer!" Isaiah 65:25 (NLT)

The world, our past, and even well-meaning fellow believers will try to caution against "believing too much."

What does that even mean???

He's God, for crying out loud!!

He can we believe in Him too much??

I'm as guilty as anyone else of this. I "don't want to get my hopes up." Good grief! How totally faithless is that??

For a brief time, I had the honor of knowing an incredible woman, the sister of a dear friend. Linda's life was not easy. She lost her husband early, she battled serious health issues her whole life, she left us too soon. At the celebration of her life, her words were printed in the order of service:

> "I HATE the words, 'Don't get your hopes up.'
> Why shouldn't I? Will lowering my expectations
> make grief or hardship easier to bear? No, and
> hope<u>less</u>ness is harder to endure than any

difficulty. Hope is a blueprint for my Faith. Hope erects a frame to which the substance of my Faith is attached.

So I will raise my hopes as high as I can get them, support them with the Word of God, and soar as long as it takes me to see them come to pass."

I have a friend, a brilliant, talented man, who became a Christian in his 30's. As he began to read and study the Bible, it never occurred to him that God wouldn't keep His promises, that he couldn't believe that what the Bible says is true.

Over 20 years later, he still believes.

Life throws us all curve balls. We don't always, with our human eyes and battle-scarred hearts, see "all things working for good." That doesn't mean they aren't, because God's Word promises they will. It just means we can't see it. Yet.

As scary and, to some, foolhardy, as it seems, I want to be that "simple soul" who picks up the Bible and believes it. I want to get my hopes up. I want to believe too much.

So, how do I do that?

First, I confess my lack of faith and my unbelief.

Then, I pray, like the father of the dying child in Mark 9:24 (ESV), *"I believe; help my unbelief!"*

And then I start. I start reading His promises. I start claiming His truth. I start rebuking Satan (and well-meaning friends) who tell me I can't or shouldn't believe.

And I start looking for His answers. They may not look like I think they will; I can almost guarantee they won't. But I will claim the answers and praise God for His faithfulness.

We see what we're looking for. If I look for answers, if I look for the truth of His Word, that's what I'll see.

I'm sure I won't get this right all the time. There'll be times I'll listen to the wrong voices. But I will, with time, find my way back to getting my hopes up. I will find my way back to the God Who is faithful and trustworthy.

And it will be amazing.

Move The Mountain

"The Lord our God said to us at Horeb, 'You have stayed long enough at this mountain.'" Deuteronomy 1:6 (NIV)

I don't know what's going on in your life, but we've gone through a stage where we were stuck at the base of "this mountain" for a very long time. We tried going over it, around it, and through it, with no obvious progress.

In Matthew 21:21-22 (NIV), Jesus told His followers, *"Truly I tell you, if you have faith and do not doubt, not only can you do what was done to the fig tree, but also you can say to this mountain, 'Go, throw yourself into the sea,' and it will be done. If you believe, you will receive whatever you ask for in prayer."*

So, we did that. We prayed in Jesus' name for the mountain to be cast into the sea. We saw opportunities that we were sure would prove to be the mountain falling into the sea. But the mountain still stood.

We are an impatient people. We microwave, we Google, we fast-lane our lives. We have lost the art of slow. We have become people who demand, "bottom-line it, give me the answer, so I can move on."

We hear but we don't listen.

We gain knowledge but not wisdom.

God doesn't work, much to our dismay, on our time schedule. We come to Him, over and over, with our requests, asking for—demanding—quick, easy answers. And when we don't get them, we decide He's not listening or He doesn't care.

But nothing could be further from the truth. God loves us; He **adores** us! What we fail to see, in our rush to grab our miracle and move on is this:

God is just as interested in the journey as He is the destination. There are always lessons to be learned along the way to His answer.

When Jesus promised us that we could move mountains, there's one thing He did not promise.

He did not promise how fast the mountain would move.

Ponder that for a while. We pray for the mountain to move. It doesn't move. So, what do we do? Do we keep believing, trusting that God is big enough and loves us enough to move the mountain? Or do we give up and walk away? He said that if we believe, the mountain will move. But maybe before it moves, He has something else in mind.

Maybe He wants us to take our eyes off the mountain and put them on the Mountain Mover.

Psalm 121 (NASB) declares,

"I will lift up my eyes to the mountains—where does my help come from?

My help comes from the Lord, who made Heaven and earth.

He will not allow your foot to slip; He who keeps you will not slumber."

When we take our eyes off the mountain, we see the One from whom our help comes. When we fix our gaze on Him, the mountain may still be there, but we now focus on the One Who will move it.

The Israelites learned a lot of lessons at the base of that mountain. They learned the cost of disobedience, they learned the power of redemption. And they learned the strength of their God. They took their eyes off the mountain and put their focus where it belonged—on their loving, providing Father.

For forty years, they sat in the shadow of that mountain. God taught them and protected them and blessed them and loved them.

In God's due time, He declared to His people, "You've been here at this mountain long enough. My purpose for your time here has been accomplished. Let's go."

In Deuteronomy 2:7 (NIV), Moses reminded the Israelites: *"The Lord your God has blessed you in all the work of your hands. He has watched over your journey through this vast desert. These forty years the Lord your God has been with you, and you have not lacked anything."*

Maybe you're still sitting at the base of your mountain. Maybe you've commanded it to be cast into the sea over and over and yet there it sits. It's keeping you in "this vast desert."

Lift up your eyes. Take them off the mountain. Lift them to the Maker of Heaven and earth. Remind yourself that He never slumbers, He is working all things for your good and that in due time the mountain **will** move.

Remember that He is watching over your journey and that it has a purpose. And rejoice that our Savior has promised that the mountain will move—in His good time.

Surrendering All

"Commit your work to the Lord, and your plans will be accomplished." Proverbs 16:3 (ESV)

As I started my day, I again asked God to show me what it was that He wanted me to do. He has a purpose for my life, a calling, a plan, and it's time I stop playing and begin living the life to which He's called me.

I've always struggled with fear, the fear of so many things. But as I examine my walk with the Lord, I realize it's not fear that holds me immobile—it's laziness. Answering His call for my life requires commitment and time and a dedicated life. Stepping into my calling has been slow and shallow and uncommitted. God wants more from me. The question I want to settle is, "Do I want more from and for me?" Do I just say the words but not mean them? Of course, the fear I have—that most of us have—is that we'll hand our lives over to God, move toward His calling, and then never get the "desires of our hearts." I know if that happens, He'll be more than sufficient. I also know that if I don't surrender—"seek ye first the kingdom of God"—I'll never get my heart's desire. It's so very hard to let go and freefall into His arms, His plan. This is my dilemma.

So, I try to articulate my fears. Somehow, I know that pulling them out of their shadowy stronghold and pushing them, kicking and screaming, into God's light, will conquer them. They have been a part of me for so long, I'm not sure how to voice them. But I pray. I tell God that I know He is sufficient, that He is enough.

We sing, "I surrender all," but I don't want to surrender all. Sadly, I fear I want what I want, small as it may be, more than I want all of God. And I acknowledge my fear—so deep inside of me—that tells me that if I do surrender all, God won't answer the way I want Him to answer. I feel somewhat ashamed (and should feel more ashamed) that I feel this way.

Satan has buried that fear deep within me, but I am the one who has fed and nurtured it. Now I want it gone, uprooted and destroyed. I want to come to the place of serving God for the sake of serving Him, not for what He'll give me for serving Him.

So, I start by asking God to reach deep into the recesses of my heart and mind and soul and free me from these fears and doubts that Satan has planted so deeply within me. I picture those precious nail-scarred hands dragging out these demons of doubt and fear and loneliness and laziness and flinging them into the pits of Hell. I feel almost ill as I realize and face what has been buried so deeply in me. I ask that it be gone.

But I also know it has to be replaced with something else, something holy and righteous, so there is no room for that evil to return. So, I ask, "Father, fill me with Your love and mercy and grace and righteousness and peace and purpose and joy. Fill me with the strength and conviction and purpose to embrace the life to which You've called me."

I've read Romans 8:38 for years—

"And I am convinced that nothing can ever separate us from God's love. Neither death nor life, neither angels nor demons, neither our fears for today nor our worries about tomorrow— not even the powers of hell can separate us from God's love." Romans 8:38 (NLT)

—but only now do I really see the truth of what Paul is saying—*life* really cannot separate me from the love of God in Christ Jesus. That's my biggest obstacle-**life** separating me from God. The day-to-day stuff. That's what keeps me from God.

Thankfully, it doesn't keep Him from me.

Standing Still

"Therefore, put on the full armor of God, so that when the day of evil comes, you will be able to stand your ground, and after you have done everything, to stand." Ephesians 6:13 (NIV)

Standing is hard. It means you're not moving and if you're a control freak like me, it means you're not getting something to happen. It means—and I cannot stress enough how horrifying this is to a control freak—that someone else is in charge.

I've never been good at just standing—or sitting. But sometimes, that's all I can do. When I've voiced every request, when I've banged on the doors of Heaven and explained to God in excruciating detail what I want Him to do, all I can do is stand. Sometimes, that's all any of us can do.

Psalm 46:10 (NIV) says, *"Be still and know that I am God."*

Exodus 14:13 (NLT) says, *"Moses answered the people, 'Do not be afraid. Just stand still and watch the Lord rescue you today. The Egyptians you see today will never been seen again.'"*

And II Chronicles 20:17 (NLT) says, *"You will not have to fight this battle. Take your positions, then stand still and watch the Lord's victory. He is with you, O people of Judah and*

Jerusalem. Do not be afraid or discouraged. Go out against them tomorrow for the Lord is with you!"

Struggling with standing still isn't a new problem. Scripture is full of stories of those who didn't wait, took matters into their own hands and really screwed up. So is my life. And so is yours.

We live in a world where the motto seems to be, "if you want it done right, do it yourself." But what happens when we can't do it ourselves or we do it ourselves and it doesn't help, or it gets worse?

We've all trusted others to help us, only to have them let us down. It's hard, in our humanness, not to expect God to do the same.

But that's not how God works.

The verse from Exodus comes right before the Red Sea parts, the Israelites cross over, and the whole Egyptian army is drowned.

The verse in II Chronicles comes right before the Lord defeats the enemies of Judah and Jerusalem without them lifting a finger.

God answers. He moves. But sometimes He doesn't move until we stop moving.

He does, of course, call on us at times to move, to pray like it all depends on Him and work like it all depends on us. And in those times, we move, we work, we pray.

But then there are those times when no amount of work seems to make a difference. Nothing in our strength changes the circumstances. We can't part the sea; we can't defeat the army. We have to stand still.

It's tempting at those times to succumb to anxiety and panic. We aren't used to being still! It'll all fall apart if we don't keep moving!

God reminds us, *"For My thoughts are not your thoughts, neither are your ways My ways."* Isaiah 55:8 (NIV)

His way of answering seldom looks the way we think it should. So often we forget that. Even while we're trying to sit still, to stand, we're trying to direct God's answer.

It doesn't work. It doesn't stop us from trying; it just doesn't work.

God promises He'll answer our prayers because He loves us. But that's not the only reason. He answers our prayers in His time—and in His way—to bring glory to His name.

We control freaks forget sometimes, in our ever-failing attempts to run the world, that we are not God. Or even God-ish. We have to be reminded that we aren't in charge. We have to stand still and **know** He is God. And sometimes we only get that message when the problems we're facing are so out of control that we have no choice.

So, stand still. Fight the anxiety and panic. And trust He is Who He says He is and He will do what He says He'll do.

The answer is coming. He will be glorified. And we will be reminded—again—that it's okay to stand still and see the glory of the Lord.

Waiting

"And let us not grow weary in doing good, for in due season we will reap if we do not give up." Galatians 6:9 (ESV)

"Humble yourselves, therefore, under the mighty hand of God so that at the proper time He may exalt you, casting your anxieties on Him, because He cares for you." I Peter 5: 6-7 (ESV)

Like 99.9% of us, I hate waiting. Anywhere. Any time. I'm not sure why it's so hard for us to wait; it's not like, for most of us, it would matter if we were five minutes later getting to our next destination. Where we will probably wind up waiting.

This is not a new problem. Frustration with waiting did not start with our generation. Look at Abraham. We all know the story. God promised him and Sarah a son. Abraham and Sarah decided God was taking too long. Hagar and Ismael enter the picture. And we're still feeling the repercussions of those choices.

In his book, *Draw the Circle: The 40-Day Prayer Challenge*, Mark Batterson says, "We're often so anxious to get out of difficult, painful or challenging situations that we fail to grow through them. We're so fixated on getting out of them that we don't get anything out of them. We fail to learn the lessons God is trying to teach us or cultivate the character God is trying to grow in us. We're so focused on God changing our circumstances that we never allow God to change us! So instead of ten or twenty years of experience, we have one year of experience repeated ten or twenty times."[19]

Ouch.

I've been there. I may be there again, but I hope not. I hope that as I move forward, I will keep asking, "Get me through this," instead of "Get me out of this."

The first time I prayed that prayer, I was in the midst of a great crisis. It took me months to get to that place of surrender. It's sad that it took that long but at least I got there. And while it didn't change the circumstances, it certainly changed my heart. Now, instead of lamenting how long the journey is taking (at least most days), I look back and see God's hand, provisions and protection. So many of the conversations between my husband and me start with, "If God had said 'yes' at the beginning, we would have never seen or known this." Every step, every apparent setback has been a gift from God.

David was somewhere between 10 and 15 years old when he was appointed king by Samuel. He didn't take the throne until he was 30. He waited between 15-20 years and spent a lot of that time running and hiding from Saul who wanted him dead.

God used those years to teach a shepherd boy how to lead. He taught him compassion and dependence on God. And David became a man after God's own heart (I Samuel 13:14 (NIV); Acts 13:22 (NIV)). This doesn't mean David didn't cry out for God to rescue him—read the book of Psalms. It means David learned he could totally depend on God to get him out—and through—his trouble.

Joseph was sold into slavery and then falsely imprisoned. He waited at least two years (some records say it could have been closer to 11 years) to be freed. The boy who bragged to his brothers about how they would bow down to him came out of prison the man who was able to say, *"You intended to harm me, but God intended it for good. He brought me to this position so I could save the lives of many people."* Genesis 50:20 (NLT)

I'm sure Joseph cried out to God to get him out of his circumstances. But instead, by getting him *through* them, God trained up a wise and compassionate leader.

In the midst of our struggle, in the darkest hours before the dawn, it's hard to remember and cling to Romans 8:28 (NIV): *"And we know that God causes everything to work together for the good of those who love God and are called according to His purpose for them."*

But it's true. He is working everything for our good. The journey may seem long and very confusing. The wait may seem like it's never, ever going to be over.

But it will. God is working in us and through us during the wait. We will survive. And, if we yield to His plan, surrender to His love and wisdom, we will come through it, knowing the wait was worthwhile.

As I Grow

"But seek first the kingdom of God and His righteousness, and all these things will be added to you." Matthew 6:33 (ESV)

I'm the first to admit that the past few years have given me great learning experiences in my walk with the Lord. And while I've learned some, I am light years from where I want or need to be.

The walk has been filled with struggles, amazing victories and many, many tears. I have walked forward, fallen back and moved again. Some days I wonder if I'll ever get it right; there are days when I am amazed at all the Father has shown me.

Here are few things I've learned:

- It's very seldom, if ever, about the answer to my prayers; it's about the journey to the answer.
- The answer is almost never the answer I envisioned.
- It's always better.
- My daily time of reading, writing and praying never goes the way I think it should or will go.
- It's always better.
- The longer I'm on this journey, the more I want to continue.

- My heart and vision have changed so much during this time.
- It's still not enough.
- While many things in me have been changed, cast out, and/or replaced, there is still so much that needs to happen within me.
- As a believer, every place I step, stand or sit is Holy Ground.
- I seldom live as if it is.
- I want to.

I'm sure the list of what I haven't learned could fill the Library of Congress!

I'm finding that the more I know about the Father, my Savior, and the Holy Spirit, the more I want to know. I feel like I've been given one of those little sample cups you get at the grocery store with just a smidgen of the best ambrosia ever created and now I'm in search of the Motherlode. I want to gorge myself on Him.

Except when I don't. I still have way too many times of distraction and wandering and disobedience. There are still too many times when I don't seek Him first—or sometimes at all.

This is what I know I want (or at least what I want to want):

- To turn, always, first to the Lord when there are crisis or decisions to make, or great need. I want Him to be my default, not my back-up plan.
- To hunger for His Word. I read books on prayer and spiritual growth. I look up verses when I write (and struggle not to feel smug that I remember some part of some verse that fits) but that's sporadic and quick. I want to want to dig in and really read and absorb into my mind, heart and soul what He has to say.
- To pray for others as much as, if not more than, I do for my husband and me
- To praise more
- To thank more

- To be quiet, to be still and really, really feel and hear Him
- To unashamedly share with others Who He is
- To seek out my friends and *hear* them when they share with me
- To judge less and love more

The journey we are all called to travel is always filled with surprises, detours, and roadblocks. Very few days are completely smooth sailing. I want to start seeing each new day as the gift that God intends it to be. I may not get it right today, but it won't stop me from trying.

So, tomorrow, I'll start again. I'll dig into His Word, I'll spend time talking to the Father, and listening for His answers. Over time, as this journey continues, I'm sure these lists will look very, very different. I'm also sure of this:

Every day is a blessing; every chance to pray is a privilege; every word I write is a gift.

Holy Ground

"Do not come any closer," the Lord warned. *"Take off your sandals, for you are standing on holy ground."* Exodus 3:5 (NLT)

"The commander of the Lord's army replied, 'Take off your sandals, for the place where you are standing is holy.' And Joshua did so." Joshua 5:15 (NIV)

Holy Ground. We're raised to believe it's inside a church. We whisper when we enter great cathedrals. It just seems to feel different when you're inside a sanctuary.

The Old Testament is full of examples of places marked by men to represent encounters with God. From Abraham, Isaac and Jacob, Moses, Joshua, and the prophets, Old Testament men of God built altars to remember God and honor His works and provision. These altars all marked Holy Ground, places where God had made His presence known.

Recently, I read again about the Holy Ground encounters of Moses and Joshua. One marked the beginning of the rescue of God's people; the second marked the end of their journey to their new home. Moses led them out; Joshua led them in.

Both encountered God and stood on Holy Ground. They took off their shoes and stood on ground declared holy by God. God met them on that Holy Ground.

When the temple of God was built, God's spirit dwelled in the Holy of Holies, the inner sanctuary, and only the High Priest could enter and then only on the Day of Atonement after careful preparation. This was the most Holy Ground. There was a huge veil that separated the Holy of Holies from the people. They could not enter; they couldn't stand on that Holy Ground.

On the day of Jesus' crucifixion, the Bible tells us that the veil that separated the people from God's presence was ripped in half from top to bottom. This veil, 60 feet high, 30 feet wide, and four inches thick, was torn apart by the hand of God. No longer would anything separate us from His presence.

I Corinthians 3:16 (NIV) says, *"Don't you know that you yourselves are God's temple and that God's Spirit dwells in your midst."*

So, now, the presence of God dwells in **us**. The temple, the Holy of Holies, is **us**. And where the presence of God is—that's Holy Ground. **We** are standing on Holy Ground. Standing, sitting, lying, walking, talking on Holy Ground.

Psalm 139:5 (NIV) declares, *"You hem me in behind and before and You lay Your hand upon me."*

We are the temple, the sanctuary of God. He surrounds us, He lays His hand on us. We are Holy Ground.

I don't always live like it. I don't live as if the very presence of God is within me. The voices of the world, the doubts and fears and anxieties push against the temple walls and I stare at them rather than at His Holy presence. Most days, folks can't look at me and say, *"Surely the Lord is in this place."* Genesis 28:16 (NIV)

I want to do better. I want to offer God a place where He can dwell and I can reflect more of Him and less of me.

When Moses came down from Mt. Sinai, his face glowed so from the glory of the Lord that he had to cover it so the people could look at him. How cool would it be to be so filled with His Spirit, His presence, that people could only see His glory?

This morning, as I worshipped and prayed, I asked the Father to make our home—here and wherever we ultimately wind up and every place in between—Holy Ground.

I pray that those who enter will know that they are standing on Holy Ground, in the presence of Almighty God. I pray that we will always remember that He is wherever we are and wherever He is, is Holy Ground.

Thank You for dwelling in me—in us. Thank You that this is—that I am—Your Holy Ground.

The Morning Song

"For you shall go out in joy and be led in peace; the mountains and the hills before you shall break forth into singing, and all the trees of the field shall clap their hands." Isaiah 55:12 (ESV)

As I'm sitting on the front stoop this morning, I hear the trill of the first bird. I'm sure there are countless folks who would know the name of that bird and maybe even why hers is the first song we hear. All I know is her song starts my day.

I can't say for sure, but I'm pretty confident that her short, sweet song was a prayer to her Creator. She started her day with a song of praise.

It made me think about how I start my day. I'd love to say I start each day reading my Bible and praising, but many, if not most, mornings are filled with prayers of petition and want. I try to do better. I try to start with praise and Bible reading.

But am I more in tune with God? Has this become my morning classroom or workroom, not my morning worship? Do I come into His presence with thanksgiving? Do I make a joyful noise to Him with songs of praise? (Psalm 95:2 ESV)

I sit here this morning, watching through the barely lit dawn, as a bunny eats breakfast next door. I listen to rain dripping from rooftops and trees. I look way overhead and see the moon reflecting down, clouds drifting over its face.

And every human part of me strains with the need to get moving, to start my daily prayers, to get through and get on with my day. I have my prayer routine. I go over my list of requests, reminding God, yet again, of our needs. I'm at old pro at repeating prayers over and over and somehow being so caught up in my prayer routine that I forget that God is anything but routine. But a little bird reminded me this morning.

So, I pause. I decide to just talk to Him about these requests. What does He think about what's on my list? What fascinating, unexpected ways will He answer? What should we be doing to get ready for His answers?

A second birdsong of the morning rings out and I almost miss it. I look up to find a bird sitting in the drive. My bunny finishes his breakfast.

There's a hush this morning, the clouds cushioning the start to the day. As dawn begins to brighten the sky, I stop and dedicate my morning, my day to my Creator. I sit and listen to the day begin. I read Psalms and hear afresh the songs of praise written so long ago and rejoice in their nearness this day.

My needs are still here; my requests are still real. I'll get to them.

But for now, I just want to remember how unexpectedly beautiful my Lord is and how blessed beyond measure I am to get to start my day with Him.

Living In Saturday

"But those who wait for the Lord shall renew their strength; they shall mount up with wings like eagles; they shall run and not be weary; they shall walk and not faint." Isaiah 40:31 (ESV)

Not too long ago, I heard a rather unconventional Easter sermon. Instead of focusing on the cross and resurrection, the pastor talked about what Saturday must have been like for the disciples. He pointed out that Friday was a pretty rough day for all of them—a lot of bad things went on. But then Saturday came. And there was silence.

I've been living in a lot of Saturdays lately, where I thought, 'I know what You said, I know Who You are, but You're awfully quiet right now. And I really need to hear from you.' We've all been there. We've walked in great victory, we've felt so close to Jesus, we could almost see the dust on his feet. But then, things change. The days get long and dark. We're filled with confusion and fear. It gets very, very quiet. It's Saturday.

So, what am I—what are you—supposed to be doing on Saturday?

The pastor said, "Saturday was the day when the roots were going down. We don't know what's going on where we can't see it."

We don't know what happened in the tomb on Saturday. Scripture doesn't tell us. A lot of people ask, a lot of people speculate. We don't need to know, or it would have been revealed to us.

But we've all had Saturdays. You may be going through a Saturday right now. I know I've been through a lot of Saturdays.

A part of Saturday is learning to be still and let God do what God needs to do.

During a hot summer several years ago, I wanted to buy and plant a dogwood tree in my yard. I went to the nursery and told the guy what I wanted to do and he said, "No, you really don't. This isn't when you want to plant a tree."

"But," I said, pointing to all trees all around me. "You have all these trees."

He shook his head. "You don't plant a dogwood tree in the summer time. You wait until right after the first frost. You want the tree to have all winter long for the roots to get long and deep so the tree will be ready for the heat."

And that's what Saturday is. That's the day the roots start going long and deep. It's the day we get ready for the heat. It's the day we get ready for what's going to come on Sunday.

And as hard as it is at times, when we're standing in Saturday and we've stood in Saturday, and we've sat in Saturday, and we've prayed in Saturday, and we've knelt in Saturday, we've raised our hands and praised on Saturday, and we've done everything we can on Saturday, and there's nothing but quiet, there's only one thing we can do.

Remember that Sunday's coming.

God never meant for us to stay in Saturday. Saturday is temporary.

We don't know what the disciples did on Saturday, except that they gathered together. And that's part of it for us—you don't isolate yourself. You gather together with others who may or may not be going through their own Saturdays (if they're not going through Saturday right now, they certainly will be again). And together, we wait for Sunday.

So, I don't know about y'all, but I'll say this, because I need to hear it and I think a lot of the rest of us do, too.

Always remember that Sunday is coming. And it will be that much sweeter because of Saturday.

The Price God Paid

"For God so loved the world that He gave His One and Only Son, that whosoever believed in Him shall not perish but have eternal life. For God did not send His Son into the world to condemn the world, but to save the world through Him." John 3:16-17 (NIV)

Several years ago, I heard a line that really hit home: "I knew Jesus loved me; I just wasn't so sure about His Dad."

For most of my life, this was my view of God. I grew up singing "Jesus Loves Me," and hearing sermons about the wrath of God. Jesus was my friend; God was my judge.

Just hearing the word "judge" tends to make us nervous. Even if we're innocent, the idea of standing before that imposing bench fills us with great anxiety, because we know that even if we're not guilty of the offense that brought us into the courtroom, we are certainly guilty of plenty of other things.

We read John 3:16-17 and think about the great sacrifice of Jesus for each of us. And it was—we will never, ever be able to wrap our minds around the price He paid for us.

But think about the first part of verse 16: *For <u>God</u> so loved the world that <u>He gave</u> His One and Only Son...* (emphasis added). Jesus willingly came. But <u>God</u> <u>sent</u> His Son.

It was a horrible sacrifice for Jesus—He left His home, lived a limited, earth-bound life, surrounded by people *He* created, abusing the precious world He had given them. Misunderstood, hated, lied about, tortured, deserted, and killed.

Now, think about His Dad.

I don't have children of my own but I have two nephews who are the sons of my soul. They own my heart and, next to my husband, there is no one I love more. Nothing has created more violent tendencies in me than some girls breaking their hearts, or someone saying or doing something to hurt them. All of nature is the same—come after our kids, you come after us.

But I also know there are times I have to stand by and let them hurt. Getting their hearts broken is a part of growing up. They have to live in this world; they will get hurt. Both nephews are now fathers and they are beginning to understand this. There is no greater pain than watching one you love hurt.

And that's what God did. He sent His most beloved One here, knowing what would happen, how bad it would be. Then He had to stand there and watch it happen, over and over.

Why? Because He loves us.

I John 4: 9-10 (NIV) says, *"This is how God showed His love among us: He sent His One and Only Son into the world that we might live through Him. This is love: not that we loved God, but that He loved us and sent His Son as an atoning sacrifice for our sins."*

And Romans 5:8 (ESV) declares, *"But <u>God</u> shows <u>His</u> love for us in that while we were yet sinners (haters of God) Christ died for us."* (Emphasis added)

I don't know about you, but I'm pretty sure I couldn't sacrifice my nephews for someone who loved me. I absolutely could not send them to be harmed—or killed—for someone who hated me.

And yet God did.

While we were still sinning. Even knowing how many times—even after we become Christians—we'd turn our backs on Him and hurt Him, and betray Him, He loved us enough to send His Son to die for us. He gave His Son in exchange for us.

We live in a fallen world. No matter how hard we try, we love imperfectly while we're here. We lash out, we fight, we hurt those we love.

But God's love is perfect. There is no losing His temper, there are no harsh, impulsive words thrown at us.

I John 4:18a (NIV) states, *"There is no fear in love. But perfect loves (God's love) drives out fear, because fear has to do with punishment."* (note added)

We are loved—by Jesus and His Dad. Before He breathed the first breath of life into Adam, God knew what it would cost His Son—and Him.

And yet he loved us enough to fill Adam's lungs with life and say, "It is very good." (Genesis 1:31 NIV)

Some days I still struggle with this. I mess up—often—and wonder how God can keep loving me. But then, He reminds me that He knew, before the beginning of time, all about my imperfections and sins. He looked through time and space and saw each of us, and said to His Son, "I'm sending You for that one, and that one, and that one. I love them. Go, make sure they have a way Home."

He loved us, even when we hated Him. He continues to love us, even when we continue to hate Him.

There is no greater love than the love of God.

"See what great love the Father has lavished on us, that we should be called the children of God! And that is what we are!" I John 3:1a (NIV)

Why We Praise

"As for me, I will always have hope; I will praise you more and more." Psalm 71:14 (NIV)

Praising God sounds so simple and yet I'm guessing that most of us, if we're completely honest, would say it's the smallest part of our prayer lives.

We all know there are days when it's pretty hard to find reasons to praise. Money's tight or nonexistent; the car won't start; the job, if we have one, stinks. We may be in the darkest pit of our lives—the diagnosis, the divorce papers, the funeral. We may be living in the dankest, dirtiest dungeon with no sign of a way out. And if you're not in that place, I hate to break it to you, you will be.

So why should we praise God in times like these?

Acts 16:25 (NIV) tells us that, *"About midnight, Paul and Silas were praying and singing hymns to God, and the other prisoners were listening."*

Paul and Silas are in prison. They have been stripped, beaten with rods, and severely flogged. Now they're in a cell, their feet in stocks.

And they start to pray and sing hymns. They get the attention of the other prisoners. But they got the attention of Someone else as well.

Acts 16:26 (NIV) says, *"Suddenly, there was such a violent earthquake that the foundations of the prison were shaken. At once all the prison doors flew open, and everyone's chains came loose!"*

Paul and Silas kept praising until Heaven responded. And boy, how Heaven responded! **Everyone's** chains came loose!

So, I'm sure that while we're in our prison, while we're in our chains, we too, should be praising. And here are some reasons why:

First, if we want victory, real, deep in our spirit, beyond a shadow of a doubt, victory, praise Him! Notice the verse doesn't talk about complaining, wailing over their misfortune, or reasoning with the guard (or God). The verse says they were "praying and singing hymns." I'm going to bet these were prayers of God's strength, protection, and provision. These were prayers that got the attention of all the other prisoners.

And they sang. Hymns of victory, hymns of the wonders of God, that told stories of all His marvelous works.

Whining and complaining doesn't get anyone's attention. But pray and praise and sing in the middle of your trial and see who notices.

Second, praising God frees us—and others. Acts 16:26 says the prison doors "flew open" and "everyone's chains came loose."

You want prison doors to fly open? Stop talking about your prison and start praising God for your freedom. You want your chains loosed? Stop looking at the chains and start looking up at the Chain Breaker. Yes, you're in a horrible, terrifying place. And yes, you want out. But if we truly want to be more when we get out of the prison and chains, we have to praise while we are in the prison and chains!

Praising while in our prison and chains does not feel natural. Our instinct is to pray with demands and pleas, reminding God, in case He's forgotten, of the horrible place we're in and how desperately we want out. It certainly doesn't feel like a place or time for praising and singing. We feel alone, forgotten, and stuck and praying, and singing and praising seem like the most illogical response imaginable.

Which brings me to the third point.

God inhabits the praises of His people.

Psalm 22:3 (CSB) declares, *"But You are holy, O You that inhabit the praises of Israel."* [20]

God was right there, in the middle of their songs and praises. Prison may not seem like a place to find God, but there He was. The power of the Almighty surrounded them. Paul and Silas began to pray and sing. Heaven responded with a violent earthquake that freed them all.

Praising in the midst of our troubles, hurts, and fears seems counterintuitive. Nothing about it seems natural. God can sometimes seem very illogical. But He calls us to praise in the storm, to pray in the darkness and to sing in the fear. And in our praising and singing, Heaven responds and frees us.

To the world, we may seem foolish. Why on earth would we sing and praise while in our prison and chains?

I Corinthians 1:27 (NIV) says, *"Instead God chose things the world considers foolish in order to shame those who think they are wise. And he chose things that were powerless to shame those who are powerful."*

We don't know who's watching us. We don't know who will be shamed or amazed by what they see. We do know that God can and will use us to reach others.

If you read the rest of Acts 16, you'll see that when the jailor woke up and saw that the doors were all open, he started to kill himself. But Paul stopped him and in short order, led him and his entire household to salvation.

So, while you're in your prison and chains, keep praising. Keep singing. Keep expecting Heaven to draw near. You never know how the chains will fall, how the doors will open. You never know who's watching. And you never know who will be changed.

All because we praise.

Even If

"Why, my soul, are you downcast? Why so disturbed within me? Put your hope in God, for I will yet praise Him, my Savior and my God." Psalm 42:5 (NIV)

The group MercyMe has a song entitled "Even If."[21] A line in the chorus proclaims:

> "But even if You don't
> My hope is You alone."

I love the song for its beautiful, painful honesty. But for a while when it first came out, I didn't listen to it. To me, those words sounded like we were giving God an out, that we were hedging our bets just in case He didn't answer our prayers according to our plan or vision.

It sounded like a pretty faithless approach to God.

The Bible is full of verses about God answering our prayers when we pray, believing. And we should; we should pray believing God is going to answer. Because the truth is, He does. Always.

But the Bible never says how He'll answer.

Isaiah 55:9 (NIV) says, *As the heavens are higher than the earth, so are my ways higher than your ways and my thoughts than your thoughts.*

His ways are higher; His thoughts are higher. Higher means better.

When my husband and I went through the long, long period of his unemployment, we struggled. I struggled. With God and with my faith. I cried out, over and over for God to get us out of our mess. There were many days during that dark time when I had to choose to keep believing; I had to trust He had a plan, even if I didn't see or understand it.

He answered, but not in the way I envisioned or, truthfully, wanted.

He got us through it, not out of it.

Sometime during those days of struggle and fear, and pain, I realized the truth of Mercy Me's song. It isn't a song of faithlessness; it is indeed a song of great faith.

When the answer doesn't come in the way we needed or wanted; when the answer seems slow to arrive or, to our human eyes, doesn't seem to come at all, we have a choice. To believe or not believe. To trust or not trust.

Paul tells us that he begged God to remove "a thorn in my flesh, a messenger from Satan, to torment me."

And God's answer was no.

"But He said to me, 'My grace is sufficient for you, for My power is made perfect in weakness.'" II Corinthians 12: 7 & 9 (NIV)

The lessons learned in the waiting or in the unrecognizable answer are hard. They hurt. But when we wrestle with the seemingly unanswered prayers, we realize the truth of who God really is. He is good, He is faithful, even when we don't get our "yes." Maybe especially when we don't.

Do we still believe He is a good, loving, faithful God when we don't get the answer? Do we walk away or do we cling to Him, knowing His love and grace are always true even when we don't understand?

The bridge of the song declares,

"You've been faithful, You've been good all my days.
Jesus, I will cling to You come what may.
'Cause I know You're able, I know You're can."

So, while we wait, while we hope and pray, we hold onto the truth of Who He is.

He is faithful
He is good

Even when the answers aren't what we imagined.
"Even though the fig trees have no blossoms, and there are no grapes on the vines; even though the olive crop fails, and the fields lie empty and barren; even though the flocks die in the fields and the cattle barns are empty, yet I will rejoice in the Lord! I will be joyful in the God of my salvation!" Habakkuk 3: 17-18 (NIV)

Endnotes

1   *New International Version®*, (NIV) Copyright ©1973, 1978, 1984, 2011 by *Biblica, Inc.*® Used by permission. All rights reserved worldwide

2   Portions excerpted from "The True Story of Kudzu, the Vine that Never Truly Ate the South," by Bill Finch, *Smithsonian Magazine*, September 2015.

3   *English Standard Version®* (ESV) Text Edition: 2016. Copyright© 2001 by *Crossway Bibles, a publishing ministry of Good News Publishers.*

4   Goodman, Karon Phillips. (2002). *You're Late Again, Lord! The Impatient Woman's Guide to God's Timing.* Uhrichsville, Ohio: Barbour Publishing, Inc.

5   *New American Standard Bible* (NASB) Copyright © 1960, 1962, 1963, 1968, 1971, 1972, 1973, 1975, 1977, 1995 by The Lockman Foundation)

6   *New Living Translation*, (NLT) copyright© 1996, 2004, 2015 by Tyndale House Foundation. Used by permission of Tyndale House Publishers, Inc., Carol Stream, Illinois 60188. All rights reserved.

7   "Give Me Jesus," Afro-American Spiritual, Public Domain Unidentified.

8   "Turn Your Eyes Upon Jesus," Helen H. Lemmel, 1922, Public Domain.

9   *The Message* (MSG) Copyright © 1993, 2002, 2018 by Eugene H. Peterson.

10 *The Passion Translation* (TPT) The Passion Translation®. Copyright © 2017 by Broad Street Publishing® Group, LLC. Used by permission. All rights reserved. ThePassionTranslation.com.

11 *New King James Version* (NKJV) New King James Version®. Copyright © 1982 by Thomas Nelson. Used by permission. All rights reserved.

12 Copyright © 2018 womowev.tk. Powered by WordPress and Themelia.

13 *Turn Your Eyes Upon Jesus,* Helen Howarth Lemmel, 1922, Public Domain.

14 *Through it All,* Songwriters: Darrell R. Brown, Dennis Matkosky, Darrell Brown ©Sony/ATV Music Publishing, LLC. Kobalt Music Publishing, Ltd, Universal Music Publishing Group, BMC Rights Management

15 *Easy-to-Read Version* (ERV) Copyright © 2006 by Bible League International

16 Eldredge, John & Stasi, *Captivating,* (Nashville, TN, Thomas Nelson, Inc., 2005), 91

17 *The Living Bible* (TLB) copyright© 1971 by Tyndale House Foundation. Used by permission of Tyndale House Publishers Inc., Carol Stream, Illinois 60188. All rights reserved.

18 Leonard Ravenhill, *Why Revival Tarries,* Sovereign World, 1992, page 71.

19 Batterson, Mark, *Draw the Circle: the 40 Day Prayer Challenge* (Grand Rapids, MI, 2012), Day 4.

20 The Christian Standard Bible. Copyright © 2017 by Holman Bible Publishers. Used by permission. Christian Standard Bible® and CSB® are federally registered trademarks of Holman Bible Publishers, all rights reserved.

21 ("Even If." Sony/ATV Music Publishing, LLC, 2017; Songwriters: Bart Millard, Ben Glover, Crystal Lewis, David Garcia, Tim Timmons. As recorded: Mercy Me, *Lifer,* Fair Trade Services, LLC, 2017.)

Printed in the United States
By Bookmasters